That You May Believe

THAT YOU MAY BELIEVE

Studies in the Gospel of John

Homer Hailey

BAKER BOOK HOUSE
Grand Rapids,   Michigan

Copyright © 1973 by
Baker Book House Company

ISBN: 0-8010-4078-7

Library of Congress Catalog Card Number:
73-81248

Printed in the United States of America

To Widna, my beloved wife of these late
years, who has so completely
filled a need and
longing in
my life.

Foreword

The Gospel of John is one of the most intriguing and beautiful books in the New Testament. It does not conform to the pattern of the Synoptic Gospels, but pursues a course peculiarly its own. Its unique purpose among the other Gospels has caused it to suffer much at the hands of the higher critics and not to be appreciated as it ought to be by the average Christian.

Homer Hailey is a man unusually well qualified to write a book on the Gospel of John. Not only has he taught this book many years in the college classroom, but he is also possessed of a deeply spiritual nature which is wonderfully enhanced by his absolute confidence in the deity of Jesus. He has drunk deeply of the humble spirit of the Son of Mary, hence is able to make Him live for his readers as the Son of God.

Mr. Hailey has done a much needed work in pointing the Bible student to the true purpose of the Gospel of John. No other work on John known to me does exactly what this book does. It is written in popular rather than technical style. This will make it not only valuable to the mature Bible student but wonderfully helpful and instructive to young preachers and average Christians who are not capable of digesting and using the material of technical works on Christian evidences.

The central theme of the deity of Jesus has been beautifully captured by the writer of this book on the Gospel of John. It is a work that literally exudes a spirit of deep conviction, abiding faith, and intense devotion. It magnifies Jesus as John truly sought for Him to be magnified in the hearts and lives of Christians by that which he penned. The style of the book is terse; its argumentation logically and scripturally sound. Yet, while many works on Christian evidences are dull and tedious reading, this work is warm and vibrant and reads easily. The reading of the manuscript was not a task but a joyful and uplifting experience. It will be read with profit and interest by all who purchase it. The words of Jesus, "Blessed are they who have not seen, and yet have believed" (John 20:29), are thoroughly vindicated by this treatise on the Gospel of John. May it enrich the lives of many by deepening and strengthening their faith in Jesus of Nazareth as God's uniquely begotten Son.

James W. Adams
San Augustine, Texas

Preface

Have questions of doubt and problems concerning the deity of Christ and the inspiration of the Bible ever gripped your heart and left you uneasy and wondering? It is possible that at some time all of us have found ourselves faced with this problem of faith and doubt. At such a time let the disturbed believer or the concerned skeptic ask himself the question, "Have I honestly considered the evidence that the Bible itself presents for the deity of Christ and the inspiration of Scripture?" An individual may read the great books on apologetics and evidences and yet pass over the one Biblical book which was written for the avowed purpose of producing and sustaining faith. That book is the Gospel of John.

Many excellent commentaries, written by outstanding scholars of various faiths, exist on this profound and beloved Gospel. I feel there is little or nothing that I can add to what has been written from the commentator's point of view. Therefore, this book is not intended to be a commentary on the Gospel of John.

Other than the unique arrangement of the materials, one will probably find little in this volume that is new. The book is not written from the viewpoint of the critical scholar, steeped in the lore of ancient languages and the philosophies of the sages, though appeal is made to a few Greek words for clarity of definition; nor is it written for the scholar who already has become familiar with the purpose and content of the Gospel of John.

My purpose is to arrange in logical order the claims made by Jesus of Nazareth concerning His own deity and those made by John on His behalf, and to point out the evidence which John presented to sustain those claims. The object of the evidence is that men may believe that Jesus is the Christ, the Son of God, and that, believing, they may have life in His name. This book is written for the man or woman who seeks a more solid assurance for his faith, a more sure foundation than his traditional acceptance of the fact. Also, it is written for the student or teacher who is looking for a practical system of evidences, simple yet conclusive, which will sustain him and which he can present to the common man.

The arrangement of the subject matter will be to present first the claims made on behalf of Jesus by John in the Prologue, and second, to present the claims Jesus made on His own behalf as set forth in His teaching. This will be followed by a presentation of the evidence found in the Gospel to sustain the claims. When quotations from the Gospel itself are used, the chapter and verse(s) will be given without designating the Book of John as the source. When quotations from other books are used, the particular book will be named. Quotations are taken from the American Standard Version.

In this work I seek to show that there is no middle ground; either Jesus was the Christ, the Son of God, or He was an impostor. He was not merely a good man. If the evidence presented in this book is convincing, I shall claim no merit because it did not originate with me; it is the evidence that convinced John and others of his generation. Its power to convince is due to the fact that it is the evidence selected by the Spirit of God and recorded to produce faith in men throughout all succeeding centuries. The evidence is simple because it is built around the life of a person—that person was the Son of God. It should be convincing because there is no other answer to the great questions, "Who say ye that I am?" and "What think ye of the Christ, whose Son is he?"

I owe a special debt of gratitude to Mrs. Margie Garrett, Direc-

Preface

tor of Development of Florida College, for her gracious and most valuable help in sentence structure suggestions. Without her help many sentences would have been awkward indeed. Also, my special thanks go to Miss Mary Cannon, who so painstakingly typed and corrected the manuscript. I am grateful to my good friends, James W. Adams and Art Dowell, for reading the manuscript and offering several valuable suggestions.

The book is sent forth by the author in sincere hope that the volume will be sympathetically received by those who read it, and that it will serve to point out the divine evidence and thereby produce or strengthen faith.

Homer Hailey
Temple Terrace, Florida

Contents

PART ONE

The Claims of Jesus

The Proposition Stated

1

The proposition of the Gospel of John is clearly stated by the writer when he said, "Many other signs therefore did Jesus in the presence of the disciples, which are not written in this book: but these are written, that ye may believe that Jesus is the Christ, the Son of God; and that believing ye may have life in his name" (20:30, 31). Eternal life depends upon this faith; nothing else will do. Either Jesus is the Christ, the Son of God—all that He claimed to be—or He was and is an impostor. There is no middle ground. This is John's proposition; it is the proposition of this book.

Let nothing be assumed, but let all argument be based on the evidence presented by John the apostle. The book (Gospel of John) is here, and what is in it, is in it; it is either fact or fiction. The question of authorship of the Gospel is not under discussion; this is dealt with by the writers of introductions to the book. It was written by one who did not so much as mention his own name, but whose name has come down to us as John. The writer does not directly claim inspiration for himself in the things which he writes, but claims to write as a witness of the things of which he writes (21:24). However, he does make indirect claim to inspiration by the Holy Spirit when he quotes Jesus' promise to the eleven apostles on the night before the crucifixion, as He said of the Spirit, "ye know him; for he abideth with you (the apostles), and shall be in you" (14:17). He continued His speech to them by saying, "But the Comforter, even the Holy Spirit, whom the Father will send in my name, he shall teach you all things, and bring to your remembrance all that I said unto you" (14:26). The promise to them of the Spirit's guidance was further made when Jesus said, "Howbeit when he, the Spirit of truth, is come, he shall guide you into all the truth" (16:13). John is one of the apostles, and the author of the book was an apostle; therefore, he was directed by the Spirit. This promise and its fulfillment is further pursued in Chapter 10. The book called "the Gospel of John" is here; it shall be heard on the merit of its own content.

In determining whether the evidence for Christ's deity is valid or invalid, trustworthy or untrustworthy, reason must serve the purpose for which it was designed. The function of reason is to sit in judgment on evidence, deduce a conclusion or decision, and render a verdict of belief or unbelief in that which the evidence seems to sustain. When evidence is presented to sustain an assumed fact, the judgment which reason deduces, belief or unbelief, will depend on several factors:

1. The strength or weakness of the evidence purporting to sustain the assumed fact.

2. The clarity with which the evidence is presented.

3. The mental ability of the hearer to weigh and evaluate testimony; that is, the logical acumen with which the individual is endowed.

4. The honesty of the individual weighing the evidence.

5. The degree to which pre-accepted judgments have been planted in the mind of the individual—his background and training.

If the evidence is sufficiently strong and is clearly presented, and if the individual is honest and has the mental ability to weigh evidence, then the prejudice of pre-accepted judgments will be overcome. It may take longer for one with previously accepted conclusions to see the truth than for one without such pre-conclusions; but like the seed planted and nurtured, it should eventually mature. When the evidence is strong and properly presented and when the learner does not have the prejudices of erroneous teaching to overcome, reason can but judge, "I believe." If the evidence is weak or illogically presented, if it is based on unverified assumptions, or if the individual is dishonest or of insufficient mental ability to evaluate the evidence and to grasp its significance, the result will be, "I do not believe."

The function of reason per se is not to determine whether the fact was possible or impossible. Reason cannot determine whether one could begotten in the womb of a woman unimpregnated by the male sperm, or whether a dead body could be raised to life again. Rather, its function is to weigh the evidence that claims to sustain the facts. Reason must sit in judgment on the evidence and determine it valid or invalid, trustworthy or untrustworthy, strong or weak. When it has done this and has deduced a conclusion on the weight of the evidence, it has served its purpose. Will must then take over.

The Book of John proposes to set forth the evidence which sustains the factuality of Jesus' being the Christ, the Son of God. The evidence convinced John; it convinced others of that day; and it has been written and preserved that it may convince all who will give it fair consideration in every generation. Jesus' first requirement for faith is that the heart be honest; it was the honest and good heart that brought forth fruit (Luke 8:15). The honest heart will reach a fair conclusion.

In "the Prologue" (1:1-18), John's introduction to his Gospel, the apostle presents Jesus as God, an eternal being, and the creator of all things. Also he introduces Him as the complete revelation of God and of His grace, who came into the world to challenge darkness and death, and to meet them in a battle that leaves both groveling in complete defeat. The claims of the Prologue are worthy of careful consideration since these set the stage for the entire book.

Christ's Relation to Deity: Essence

John begins with the affirmation, "In the beginning *was* the Word" (1:1a). John takes us back to the beginning of all things, the creation of the heavens and the earth (Gen. 1:1), where he finds the Word already *was*. He, the Word, is therefore without beginning, uncreated, eternal. This Word, John declares, "became

flesh, and dwelt among us" as the only begotten Son of God
(1:14). Before the beginning of creation, He already was.

Further, He was *with* God (1:1b). The expression means more
than simple co-existence; rather, it conveys the idea of active
intercourse and communion (Westcott). The term expresses the
presence of one person with another (Dods). The Word, therefore,
is not only eternal, but also personal; He was with God before He
revealed God. Being *with* God identifies the Word as one of the
persons of the Godhead, yet one who maintains His own identity.

And more, "the Word was *God*" (1:1c). The emphasis in this
phrase is not on the word *was,* but on the word *God.* The Word
was *Deity.* John does not say the Word was *a* God, nor does he say
the Word was *the* God; he says, "the Word was *God.*" The Word
was God in His nature and in His being, possessing the fulness of
divine being, power, and attributes. The writer of Hebrews
summed up the thought when he said, "who being the effulgence
of his (God's) glory, and the very image of his substance" (Heb.
1:3). Theologians use the word *essence;* He was the very *essence* of
God. There is nothing of God that man in the flesh could comprehend or grasp of God's nature, character or being, so long as he is
in the flesh, that God has not summed up in Christ.

In His relation to Deity, He existed before creation; therefore,
He was eternal. He was with God, personal, in communion with
Him. He was Deity itself, the very image of the divine essence.

Christ's Relation to the Physical World: Creator

In His relation to the creation, John declares, "All things were
made through him; and without him was not anything made that
hath been made" (1:3). All things, taken severally, one by one,
were made by Him. He was the active agent through whom all
created beings or things came into existence. God was Creator in
the sense that He purposed and planned the creation. As the
twenty-four elders sang the song of God's praise for the creation
of all things, they said, "For thou didst create all things, and
because of thy will they were, and were created" (Rev. 4:11). All
things to be created were designed in the mind of God before they
came into existence. Their creation became an expression of His
will. It was by God's will that they were, but they were created by

Jesus Christ as the Word of God. This puts Christ before all things, both in time and in preeminence or primacy.

Christ's Relation to the Moral World: Life and Light

In passing from the universe of creation to the spiritual or moral realm, John says of Him, "In him was life; and the life was the light of men" (1:4). Life in all of its fulness and completeness was in Him. That great chasm that separates the inanimate and the animate was spanned by the Word. But more, that which separates the non-moral and the moral also was spanned by Him in whom was life. From Him proceeded the life that has given light to men, the revelation of God which appeals to the conscience and reason of man. The life not only gives light to a darkened world, but it is that which quickens in man a response to the light. Further, that "light of men" extended beyond the Jew to include the Gentile; it included all men.

Christ's Relation to Darkness: Challenger and Victor

The life "which was the light of men" was immediately challenged by the darkness: "And the light shineth in the darkness; and the darkness apprehended it not" (1:5). The marginal reading is preferable, "the darkness overcame it not." The light came into the world to challenge the darkness by illuminating every man, but from the moment of its entrance into the world there was conflict between that light and the moral darkness which for so long had held the human family captive. "The whole phrase is indeed a startling paradox. The light does not banish the darkness: the darkness does not overpower the light. The two co-exist in the world side by side" (Westcott). In this statement John introduces the conflict which is seen throughout the book. Light invades the realm of darkness and there follows the conflict between light and darkness, between truth and error, between belief and unbelief, which in the end leaves darkness, error, and unbelief thoroughly defeated.

At this point the writer introduced John the Baptist and his work. He was not the light, but his mission was to bear witness to the light. He is introduced as one sent from God, a divinely sent messenger on a divine mission. But the true light that "lighteth every man" was now coming into the world, the Word in person.

Christ's Relation to Humanity: Creator and Benefactor

Having affirmed that all things were made through Him (v. 3), John proceeded to say, "He was in the world," the sum total of created being, of which He Himself was the creator; for "the world was made through him" (1:10a), but this world did not recognize Him. He had been in it all the time, ordering, controlling, guiding, "upholding all things by the word of his power" (Heb. 1:3), as the one in whom "all things consist" (Col. 1:17). But that world, the rational world of humanity, which should have recognized Him because of a divine kinship, "knew him not" (v. 10b). Paul's affirmation is helpful in understanding this; he says, "the world through its wisdom knew not God" (I Cor. 1:21), and "that, knowing God, they glorified him not as God," for "that they exchanged the truth of God for a lie, and worshipped and served the creature rather than the Creator, who is blessed for ever" (Rom. 1:21, 25).

In a special way He had come unto His own, the Jews, but they had received Him not. But to as many as believed on Him, He had given the power or right to become children of God, children of a spiritual family (vv. 11-13). And now, as the light that lights every man, He was coming into the world to the Jews who rejected Him and to the Gentiles who in ages past had refused to have Him in their knowledge. In this statement John is affirming that in His relation to the world He is both its Creator and its Benefactor.

Christ's Relation to the Father: Revelation

It was this Word, eternal Deity, Creator, and Sustainer of the universe, who in the flesh had now come into the world. "And the Word became flesh, and dwelt among us (and we beheld his glory, glory as of the only begotten from the Father), full of grace and truth" (1:14). Here is Deity in the flesh, the manifestation of God in a visible and tangible form, the coming into this world of one from without. He "dwelt" among them. The word *dwelt* (*skēnoō*) means "to fix one's tabernacle (or tent), tabernacle" (Thayer). In the old dispensation, as the "glory," God had taken up His abode among Israel in the tabernacle (Exod. 40:34-38). So now the Word takes up His abode or tabernacle among us in the flesh. Wherefore John says, "we beheld," that is, observed, considered, had occasion to study His glory. In the things which he wrote in the remainder of his book, the apostle gives us an opportunity to behold, observe, and study this glory, so that a decision might be reached as to who He is. Also, one must determine whether or not the glory manifested in Him is worthy of that which should belong to a divine person such as He claimed to be.

In the flesh He revealed the Father: "No man hath seen God at any time; the only begotten Son, who is in the bosom of the Father, he hath declared him" (1:18). *Declared* (*exegeomai*), "metaphorically, to draw out in narrative, unfold in teaching; to unfold, to declare" (Thayer). Men had seen visions, theophanies, and angelic appearances of God; but until the advent of Jesus in the flesh, no man had seen God in person. Now "the only begotten Son," He who was with God from the beginning and who was Deity itself, has revealed, interpreted, unfolded God, becoming "a satisfying exposition" of Him.

In His relation to God the Father, He is the only begotten Son, the complete and perfect revelation of Him. In this He fulfilled the words of the prophets who had fore-declared that He should be "Immanuel"—God with us—(Isa. 7:14); God's "fellow" (Zech. 13:7); the "child . . . born," the "son . . . given," whose name should be called "Wonderful, Counsellor, Mighty God, Everlasting Father, Prince of Peace" (Isa. 9:6, 7).

Christ's Relation to Grace: Fulness

In Him we behold not only the glory as of the only begotten from the Father, but we also behold Him as one "full of grace and truth" (1:14). John further declares, "For of his fulness we all received, and grace for grace. For the law was given through Moses; grace and truth came through Jesus Christ" (1:16, 17).

Christ, the Word, is the fulness of Deity, of Godhood. The word *fulness* is used by John and by Paul with the same connotation. Paul says, "For it was the good pleasure of the Father that in him should all the fulness dwell" (Col. 1:19); and, "in him dwelleth all the fulness of the Godhead (Godhood) bodily, and in him ye are made full" (Col. 2:9, 10). Lightfoot explains the word *fulness* (*plērōma*) as "that which is completed, i.e., the complement, the full tale, the entire number or quantity, the plentitude, the perfection."[1] Hence, the plentitude, perfection, the fulness of Godhood or Deity is summed up in Christ; from Him proceeds grace and truth in its fulness and completeness. Not only are all the attributes and characteristics of God summed up in Christ, but also the completeness of Godhood itself dwelt in Him bodily (Col. 2:9). The unmerited favor of God therefore flows from Him to us.

The Question

These are the claims of the Prologue. This poses the question: Does the available evidence sustain the claims? As John presents the testimony, reason must weigh it and then determine the answer. For a possible conclusion we are left with five alternatives:

1. Jesus never lived, but was the product of the human mind, a figment of the imagination of John and other evangelists who have left records of His life and activities. However, since we are considering John's presentation of Jesus, the evidence offered by John is a product of his fervid imagination; and both the claims he made for Jesus and the evidence he offers are the product of his own unfounded fancy. Or,

2. Jesus lived, but was merely a good man, a great teacher, and a great philosopher and moralist who possessed a greater and deeper concept of God as Spirit than any who had lived before Him or after Him. Jesus was able by His own greatness and goodness to beget and develop in the minds of His disciples such a concept of Himself as presented by John. Or,

3. Jesus was not the Messiah, but as a deeply religious Jew of northern Palestine, He believed that He was. In this confidence and His thorough knowledge of the Old Covenant, He was able so to impress the naive and gullible peasants and village folk of Galilee that they, too, came to believe that He was the Christ. Or,

4. Jesus was a shrewd and cunning impostor, able to deceive John and others whom He convinced that He was the Messiah of their expectations. He becomes the arch-deceiver of history, for He so completely deceived them that millions since have been deceived and deluded by His imposture. Or,

---

1. J. B. Lightfoot, *St. Paul's Epistle to the Colossians*, p. 256.

5. Jesus was what John claimed for Him, and what He claimed for Himself: the Christ, the Son of God, the Messiah of prophecy.

When the first of these alternatives is considered, one is faced with the question of whether John was great enough to create such a character for whom he could make such claims and whether he was able to create out of his own imagination the teaching which he ascribed to Jesus. Was he able to create characters such as live in his Gospel and to array their testimony in such a way as to make his book live through the centuries? Plainly stated, which is the greater wonder: Jesus and the evidence of facts as John presented them, or the creation of such a character as Jesus and the evidence from the imagination of a Galilean fisherman? Reason must determine the answer.

The second alternative is ruled out on the ground of Jesus' claims. His claims are such that either He was the Christ or He was not a good man. Unless He was who He claimed to be, He was an impostor, a blasphemer, a hypocrite, a deceiver, and a liar. He could not falsely claim what He claimed for Himself and at the same time be a good man.

The third alternative does not explain the empty tomb, the conversion and work of Saul of Tarsus, or the impression of Jesus upon the Gentile world and upon history.

The fourth alternative leaves us with the problem of accepting the greatest concept of God and the greatest system of ethics and morals known to man as the offspring of the world's greatest fraud, deceiver, and liar. This is an absurdity, for it is an axiom accepted by all that a tree bears after its kind. Such an evil tree could not have produced such good fruit.

We are left with only the fifth alternative as one that can be accepted if it can be shown that Jesus was a good man, that He did reveal the loftiest concept of God that the world has had, and that the system of ethics and morals taught by Him are without flaw. As the evidence is presented by John and reason weighs it, the reader must determine what he shall do with Jesus. The book is here; what is in it, is in it; and it is fact or fiction. If fact, then Jesus is the Christ, the Son of God and Savior of the world. If fiction, then John has perpetrated upon mankind a fraud of gigantic proportions with no known motive for his fraud.

His Relation to God

2

The claims that Jesus made concerning Himself as set forth in the Gospel of John, if sustained, are such that prove Him to be the Son of God; if they are not sustained, they prove Him to have been the arch-impostor of history. In this and in the following two chapters the claims are presented. In these chapters no effort is made to prove the claims to be true, but the following chapters will present the evidence that John advances to sustain the claims that have been made. Jesus claimed:

That He Came from God

To Nicodemus Jesus introduced the necessity of a new birth in order to possess the rights and privileges of citizenship in the kingdom of God (3:1-8). Nicodemus then expressed difficulty in understanding the concept of a new birth (v. 9), whereupon Jesus mildly reprimanded him for not being able to understand these things. Jesus felt that, as a teacher in Israel, Nicodemus should have comprehended what He was saying (vv. 10-12). Jesus proceeded to the discussion of heavenly things by making the claim that "no one hath ascended into heaven, but he that descended out of heaven, even the Son of man, who is in heaven" (v. 13). The last expression, "who is in heaven," is probably parenthetical and is John's further explanation that one who came down out of heaven would certainly return to that realm from whence he came. Jesus here expressed His claim to the right to speak of heavenly things on the ground that He had descended out of heaven. He had come from heaven; therefore, He had brought first-hand information about all that of which He spoke.

After feeding the five thousand, Jesus delivered a discourse on the bread of life. His claims concerning Himself and His relation to this bread are significant. "For the bread of God is that which cometh down out of heaven, and giveth life unto the world" (6:33); "I am the bread of life" (6:35); "For I am come down from heaven, not to do mine own will, but the will of him that sent me" (6:38); "I am the living bread which came down out of heaven"; He assures His hearers that if anyone should eat of this bread he would live forever (v. 51). And, finally, He challenged them with the question, "What then if ye should behold the Son of man ascending where he was before?" (v. 62). These claims were too much for most of the Jews who heard Him, for "upon this many of his disciples went back, and walked no more with him" (v. 66). The twelve, however, acknowledged their faith in Him and continued with Him. In order to convince one, either then or now, that He is the bread of life that came down from heaven, the evidence must be sufficiently strong to persuade the spiritually hungry to eat.

The time of the feast of tabernacles arrived (7:2); and instead of going up to Jerusalem with His brothers, Jesus went up to Jerusalem alone after they had gone. When He arrived in the city, there was much concern about Him. Some said, "He is a good man; others said, Not so, but he leadeth the multitude astray" (7:12). In the midst of this concern over Him and in spite of the fact that the Jews sought to kill Him, He went up openly into the temple and began to teach. If He was from God as He had claimed, He must do the will of God for which He was sent. Some Jews expected their Messiah to appear suddenly, from unknown quarters (7:27), while others expected Him to come from Bethlehem, the City of David (v. 42). Jesus told them that they knew who He was, the son of Mary and of Joseph (as they supposed), and from whence He was (Nazareth), but that they did not know Him who had sent Him (7:27-28). He then made the startling claim, "I know him; because I am from him, and he sent me" (v. 29).

On the point of His witness concerning Himself, Jesus recognized that from the viewpoint of the law His witness alone would not be accepted; establishing His claims would require the witness of more than Himself only (5:31). However, the witness would be true because it would be truth; He would be speaking whereof He knew: "Even if I bear witness of myself, my witness is true; for I know whence I came, and whither I go; but ye know not whence I come, or whither I go" (8:14). Actually, they were incompetent to judge what He said, for they knew neither the things of God nor what He spoke. His witness was true, for, having come from God, He knew whereof He spoke.

Another of the startling claims of Jesus relative to His having come from God was made in the same discourse when He said, "Ye are from beneath; I am from above: ye are of this world; I am not of this world" (8:23). The Jews whom He addressed were "from beneath, of this world"; in contrast, He was "from above, not of this world." Jesus means this world of ungodly men in rebellion against God. He was in it, but not of it; He was separate from them. This suggests a question as to how He got into the world beneath, having come from another, that is, from above. Had He been born of Mary and Joseph, He would have been of this world, as they were; but since He was not of it, He must have entered it another way. In the statement Jesus infers a supernatural entrance into this world.

In the claims of Jesus considered later, He related Himself to man as one with Him. The question is posed as to how He could have been both God and man unless by the supernatural begettal in the womb of His mother. If God had created for Him a special body, He would not have been related to the descendants of Adam. If God sent an angel, it would not have been God manifest in the flesh. There is no alternative to that of the divine begettal. By it Jesus is related to God and to man. The claim indicates a special means of entrance into the world.

In the next breath Jesus affirmed the necessity of believing the fact that He is from above and not of this world; He said, "For except ye believe that I am he, ye shall die in your sins" (v. 24). If a supernatural birth is essential to His having come from above and of His being not of this world, then this must be believed if one is to avoid dying in his sins. The fact of His being from above and not of this world would be confirmed in His death. He indicated this truth when He said, "When ye have lifted up the Son of man, then shall ye know that I am he, and that I do nothing of myself, but as the Father taught me, I speak these things" (v. 28). This involves the resurrection. The resurrection, which followed His being lifted up, would be the confirming witness to His claim that He was from above and not of this world and that He had entered the world by a supernatural birth.

Finally, in the same discourse, Jesus attributed their attitude toward Him and their lack of love for Him to the fact that they did not love God and did not know Him. He said, "If God were your Father, ye would love me: for I came forth and am come from God; for neither have I come of myself, but he sent me" (v. 42).

John's own conviction, as one who had been with Him for three years and had had ample time and opportunity to observe the facts, is summed up as he describes Jesus' action at the last supper: "Jesus, knowing that the Father had given all things into his hands, and that he came forth from God, and goeth unto God," arose from the table and washed the disciples' feet (13:3). He used this as an occasion not only to teach the disciples a lesson of humility and service, but also to emphasize the necessity of moral cleanliness and to point out that one among them was not clean (v. 11).

In summary: Jesus claimed that He came from God, that He would return to God, that God had sent Him, that the bread of life which He offered the world was from God, and that He had brought it down from God. He claimed that His knowledge of God and His witness to the Father were true because of their source—they had come from above. And further, except they would believe that He was from God, from above, they would die in their sins. This makes belief in the Deity and supernaturalness of Jesus imperative to salvation from sin.

That He Alone Has Seen God

On the ground that He had come from the Father, Jesus made the claim that only He had seen the Father: "Not that any man hath seen the Father, save he that is from God, he hath seen the Father" (6:46). John himself had been impressed with this fact, for in the Prologue he had said, "No man hath seen God at any time; the only begotten Son, who is in the bosom of the Father, he hath declared him" (1:18). Paul attested to the same fact when he wrote of Him, "whom no man hath seen, nor can see" (I Tim. 6:16).

This claim made by Jesus immediately raises questions of statements found in the Old Covenant concerning God's appearances to men. God talked with Adam in Eden (Gen. 3); "Jehovah appeared to Abram" (Gen. 17:1); and "Jehovah appeared unto him (Abraham) . . . and he (Abraham) lifted up his eyes and looked, and, lo, three men stood over against him" (Gen. 18:1-2). These three men ate the food which the Patriarch prepared for them, after which Jehovah told him what He purposed to do with Sodom. Two of these men are later spoken of as "angels" (Gen. 19:1, 15). Jehovah is reported also to have appeared to Isaac and Jacob (Ex. 6:3), to Moses, and later to many others.

Of Moses Jehovah said, "with him will I speak mouth to mouth, even manifestly, and not in dark speeches; and the form of Jehovah shall he behold" (Num. 12:8). At Sinai, Moses, accompanied by seventy-three others, went up on the mount, "and they saw the God of Israel . . . and they beheld God, and did eat and drink" (Exod. 24:9-11). However, God said to Moses, "Thou canst not see my face; for man shall not see me and live" (Exod. 33:20). Jehovah then put him in a cleft of the rock, and as He passed by, Moses was permitted to see His back (vv. 21-23).

Despite the fact that in books of the Old Covenant it is said that various ones saw God, it is also said in those same books that they could not see Him. Therefore it becomes evident that what they saw was a visible means by which God chose to make Himself manifest. The manifestation might be in a burning bush, as at Sinai where He appeared to Moses, or in a pillar of cloud by day and a pillar of fire by night, as He led Israel out of Egypt. Or He might visit Abraham in the person of an angel who appeared as a man; or He might be represented by "angels" as at Sinai when He gave the law to Moses (Acts 7:53; Gal. 3:19). As He prepared to lead Israel from Sinai into Canaan, God promised that He would send one before them, "an angel . . . to keep . . . the way," one in whom God would put His name and to whom they should listen (Exod.

23:20-23). Isaiah speaks of this one who was with them in the wilderness as "the angel of his presence" (Isa. 63:9). It was in this "angel of his presence" that Jehovah had appeared to the patriarchs of old.

If evidence sustains Jesus' claim that He had come from Him, He spoke the truth when He claimed that He alone had seen God. All manifestations of God hitherto had been through angels or through other visible means by which God had sought to impress man with His presence, for no man could look upon Him and live. Now that He had manifested Himself in Jesus, His only begotten Son, the express image of Himself, Jesus could say, "He that hath seen me hath seen the Father" (14:9).

That He Knows God

The Greeks had two words which are translated into English by the word *know*. The words are *ginōskō*, "know, come to know"; and *oida,* "be (intimately) acquainted with, stand in a (close) relation to."[1]

Jesus used both words in describing His knowledge of the Father. In His discourse on Himself as the "good shepherd," He used *ginōskō*: "I am the good shepherd; and I know mine own, and mine own know me, even as the Father knoweth me, and I know (*ginōskō*) the Father" (10:14, 15). Also, in His prayer to the Father, He used the same word when He said, "O righteous Father, the world knew thee not, but I knew (*egnōn ginōskō*) thee" (17:25). In both instances Jesus used the word which describes acquired knowledge, knowledge derived by observation and experience, "knowing which is the result of discernment and which may be enlarged. This knowledge may be drawn from external facts or from spiritual sympathy."[2] As one sharing common humanity with those whom He came to save and entering into all human experience with them, Jesus would learn, come to know God by experience, as do all men. The thought suggested in both passages is that of knowledge which is intimate, direct, and personal, "both being bound together by holy and inseparable love."[3]

---

1. Arndt and Gingrich, *A Greek-English Lexicon of the New Testament,* pp. 159-160.
2. Marvin R. Vincent, *Word Studies in the New Testament,* Vol. II, p. 88.
3. Henry Alford, *The Greek Testament,* Vol. I, p. 766.

Upon other occasions Jesus used *oida,* which indicates a more absolute knowledge. In the midst of discussion as to who He was, He said of His relation to the Father, "I know (*oida*) him; because I am from him, and he sent me" (7:29). This "implies absolute knowledge: the knowledge of intuition and of satisfied conviction."[4] His origin and relation with the Father is, and has been, of such nature that Christ can claim knowledge of Him which others cannot have; He knows Him thoroughly. He was not dependent upon the same source of knowledge as were they; He brought His knowledge with Him. Here we have fulness of knowledge.

Jesus expressed this same confident and intimate knowledge when later He said, "Even if I bear witness of myself, my witness is true; for I know (*oida*) whence I came, and whither I go; but ye know not whence I come, or whither I go" (8:14). With Him the knowledge was absolute.

Again Jesus used the word *oida* when He said, "And ye have not known him: but I know him; and if I should say, I know him not, I shall be like unto you, a liar: but I know him, and keep his word" (8:55). Jesus knew (*ginōskō*) God by experience with Him through His word, by His coming to know as would all men; and He knew (*oida*) Him with an intuitive knowledge—knowledge which reflected His presence with the Father in heaven and which He brought with Him from heaven. Peter used both words of Jesus when he said, "Lord, thou knowest (*oidas,* appealing to His absolute knowledge) all things; thou knowest (perceivest, *ginōskeis,* appealing to His discernment) that I love thee" (21:17).

That He Reveals God

Out of this knowledge of God and Christ's relation to Him, Jesus claimed that in Himself was to be found a complete revelation of God. In the Prologue John had made the claim that "he (Jesus) hath declared him (God)" (1:18). As He neared the end of His ministry among men, His death already determined by the Pharisees and His Jewish followers afraid to confess their belief in Him, Jesus made one final bold claim as He cried, "He that believeth on me, believeth not on me, but on him that sent me. And he that beholdeth me beholdeth him that sent me" (12:44, 45). He followed this claim that to behold Him was to

---

4. Vincent, p. 88.

behold the Father with the additional challenging claim, "For I spake not from myself; but the Father that sent me, he hath given me a commandment, what I should say, and what I should speak . . . The things therefore which I speak, even as the Father hath said unto me, so I speak" (vv. 49-50). Hence, to behold Him was and is to behold the Father; and to hear Him was and is to hear the Father. He was the revelation both of the Father and of His word.

Shortly after this, as Jesus was observing the Passover feast with His disciples, He declared to them, "If ye had known me, ye would have known my Father also: from henceforth ye know him, and have seen him" (14:7). Philip failed to grasp the significance of the statement and made a request which sums up the desire of all human hearts through the ages: "Lord, show us the Father, and it sufficeth us" (v. 8). Jesus' reply to this request not only sums up an all-embracing claim for Himself as the revelation of God, but also implies a deep hurt at the thought that He had been among them for so long, yet even these closest to Him had failed to recognize Him. His answer was, "Have I been so long time with you, and dost thou not know me, Philip? he that hath seen me hath seen the Father; how sayest thou, Show us the Father?" (v. 9). His words were the words of His Father; His actions were the actions of the Father, as the Father in Him was doing His works (vv. 11, 12). This they should have recognized.

In these words Jesus was claiming by insinuation that in Him was the final revelation of God. For if God was in Him and if to see Him was to see the Father, there would be nothing more that God could reveal of Himself that would be comprehensive to man in the flesh. If, in Christ, God has summed up the fulness of Godhood and all the attributes of Himself in their completeness, then truly to see Him is to see the Father. The universal hunger of the human soul for a revelation of God to man is satisfied in Jesus if the evidence will sustain the claim.

It was on the ground of this claim that in Him God had made a full and complete revelation of Himself, that Jesus made the charge, "If I had not come and spoken unto them, they had not had sin: but now they have no excuse for their sin" (15:22). The specific sin to which He here referred is that of hatred for Him: "He that hateth me hateth my Father also" (v. 23). The words Jesus had taught and the works He had done were in keeping with what they should have expected of the Father; therefore, they were without excuse for their guilt. And in hating Him they were hating the Father, who, in Him, was doing His works and teaching; "but now have they both seen and hated both me and my Father" (v. 24).

That He Is Equal with God

Probably no claim made by Jesus was greater or more shocking to His hearers than the one in which He claimed equality with God. However, this should be expected in the light of the claims already presented. Jesus was in Jerusalem for one of the Jewish festivals (5:1), when, by the pool of Bethesda, He found and healed a man who for thirty-eight years had been in a state of infirmity. The Jews were incensed because the miracle was performed on a sabbath day; wherefore they charged Him with having violated the law of the sabbath. Jesus' answer to the charge was, "My Father worketh even until now, and I work" (5:17). John then adds, "For this cause therefore the Jews sought the more to kill him, because he not only brake the sabbath, but also called God his own Father, making himself equal with God" (v. 18).

The Jews correctly interpreted the words of Jesus; He claimed a special relation to God. If He could heal a lame man, it would be by the power of God; if He did it on the sabbath day, then both the work and the sabbath belonged to Him. Although the Father had rested from the work of creation, He had never stopped working. If the Father works, and Jesus works the works of the Father as the Father's "hand," then He and the Father would be equal. As a matter of fact, in this accusation they were charging the Father with having broken the sabbath.

Later, while in Jerusalem for the feast of dedication (10:22), the Jews again accosted Him, saying, "If thou art the Christ, tell us plainly" (10:24). Jesus introduced the subject of His relation to the sheep, having discussed this relationship on His previous visit to Jerusalem (10:1-16), making the claim that no one could snatch them out of His hand or snatch them out of the Father's hand. To this He added, "I and the Father are one" (10:30). The claim is more than a claim to oneness in caring for the sheep; He and His Father are two persons, but one in essence. The claim is that He is "the very image (impress) of his (the Father's) substance" (Heb.

1:3). Jesus and His Father are one in Godhood, one in purpose, and one in power; this is the claim of Jesus in His relation to the Father.

Yet, in spite of this claim, Jesus recognized that in some sense the Father was greater than He. Jesus had told the disciples that He was going away. This should have filled them with rejoicing instead of sadness, because He was going to the Father; "For," said He, "the Father is greater than I" (14:28). Luther's summary of the meaning of Jesus' words is given by Alford, "This word 'greater' is not here used as referring to the *Nature or Essence of the Son as related to the Father,*—but as indicating that particular subordination to the Father in which the Lord Jesus then was."[5] Paul sustained this point when he wrote, "who . . . counted not the being on an equality with God a thing to be grasped, but emptied himself, taking the form of a servant, being made in the likeness of men; and being found in fashion as a man, he humbled himself, becoming obedient even unto death" (Phil. 2:6-8). In all that Jesus did, He carried out the Father's will. Also, all of His teaching was the teaching of the Father. The Father was revealing Himself in Him. In Godhood they were equal; in eternal superiority, in rank, and in preeminence, the Father was greater than He.

A further recognition of His equality with the Father is revealed in His acceptance of worship from others. Jesus taught that "the true worshippers shall worship the Father in spirit and truth" (4:23, 24). Yet, when the man born blind, whose eyes Jesus had opened, was told by Jesus that He was the Son of God, the man responded by saying, "Lord, I believe. And he worshipped him" (9:38). Jesus accepted this worship as though it was in perfect order. Either He was equal with God and therefore worthy of worship, or He was a hypocrite of the darkest dye.

That He Does the Works of God—Possessing the Powers of God

The healing of the lame man by Jesus on the sabbath has been introduced above. This incident had led the Jews to charge that Jesus made Himself equal with God (5:18). Jesus countered by saying, "The Son can do nothing of himself, but what he seeth the Father doing: for what things soever he doeth, these the Son also

---

5. Alford, p. 804.

doeth in like manner" (v. 19). He further claimed that the Father shows the Son all things that the Father does; and "greater works than these will he show him, that ye may marvel" (v. 20). In the remainder of the chapter, Jesus makes some of His most stupendous claims regarding the work He had come to do.

He Would Give Spiritual Life. "For as the Father raiseth the dead and giveth them life, even so the Son also giveth life to whom he will" (v. 21). The power to give life and to raise the dead were considered by the Jews as prerogatives of God and as expressions of the highest power.[6] The life Jesus here proposes to give is spiritual life, eternal life (v. 24). This life is imparted through the hearing of His word (v. 25). This life is from God, given to the Son, and hence it would have to be eternal life, since God Himself is eternal (v. 26). Truly, this was a work of God, but a work now vested in the Son.

He Would Judge. This was a work which hitherto was the inherent prerogative of the Father only. But the Father does not now judge, "but he hath given all judgment unto the Son; that all may honor the Son, even as they honor the Father" (vv. 22, 23). To judge (*krino*) is "to pronounce an opinion concerning right and wrong . . . Of the judgment of God or of Jesus the Messiah, deciding between the righteousness and unrighteousness of men."[7] However, the primary mission of Jesus' coming into the world was not to judge but to save, for "God sent not the Son into the world to judge (condemn or inflict penalty upon) the world; but that the world should be saved through him" (3:17). By his unbelief and love for the darkness man judged (condemned) himself (3:18-20). Christ's judging would be to decide between the righteousness and unrighteousness of men as He set the standard by which these are determined; and further, He offered eternal life to men who, if they rejected it, were brought under condemnation.

This principle was further indicated by Jesus when He said, "I can of myself do nothing: as I hear, I judge: and my judgment is righteous; because I seek not mine own will, but the will of him that sent me" (5:30). And further, Jesus claimed that He came as a light into the world, that those who should believe might not abide in darkness (12:46). But here is the standard of judgment, "He that rejecteth me, and receiveth not my sayings, hath one that

---

6. Marcus Dods, *The Expositors Greek Testament*, Vol. I, p. 739.

7. Wm. Henry Thayer, *Grimm's Lexicon*, p. 361.

judgeth him: the word that I spake, the same shall judge him in the last day" (12:48). This word by which they should be judged was the word given Him by the Father (vv. 49-50).

The judgment (*krisis*), "a separating, sundering, separation; selection; judgment, i.e., opinion or decision given concerning anything, esp. concerning justice and injustice, right and wrong,"[8] would be determined by the individual's love for darkness (3:19), evil conduct (5:29), and failure to forsake the prince of this world (12:31; 16:8, 11). The judgment would be determined by the standard of truth (8:16) and righteousness (7:24). All that this work of judging involves was now His.

He Would Raise the Physically Dead, a Work Likewise Attributed to God. "Marvel not at this"—the work of giving spiritual life and of judging—"for the hour cometh, in which all that are in the tombs shall hear his voice, and shall come forth; they that have done good, unto the resurrection of life; and they that have done evil, unto the resurrection of judgment" (5:28, 29). This is a direct claim by Jesus to a bodily resurrection, both of the righteous and the wicked. This is projected into the future, "the hour (point in time) cometh" when all the physically dead shall hear and come forth. The spiritually dead are to be made spiritually alive by hearing His voice in the word of truth; the physically dead are to be brought forth by the power of that same voice, and all are to be judged by that word which He has spoken from the Father. Majestic claims, indeed! Surely He was either the Son of God or the greatest impostor the world has had to face. But the fact that the hearing of His voice has given spiritual life to millions makes it hard to believe that He is the arch-impostor of all time. There were other works which He claimed to do by the power of God, but these suffice to sustain the point.

That He Possesses the Attributes of God

A consideration of the claims of Jesus in His relation to God would be incomplete without giving attention to the various attributes of God which Jesus claimed for Himself. Four of these are considered:

Eternity. In His controversy with the Jews over the subject of the true children of Abraham, Jesus made the statement that

8. Thayer, p. 361.

"your father Abraham rejoiced to see my day; and he saw it, and was glad" (8:56). This brought forth the sharp retort from the Jews, "Thou art not yet fifty years old, and hast thou seen Abraham?" (v. 57). To this question Jesus replied, "Verily, verily, I say unto you, Before Abraham was born, I am" (v. 58). "The phrase (I am) marks a timeless existence."[9] It marks the contrast between the temporal and the eternal, between the created and the uncreated. It is a claim to eternal being; it is a clear declaration of His pre-fleshly state or existence. One is reminded of the "I AM" of Jehovah in His reply to Moses at the burning bush (Exod. 3:14), where He declared Himself to be the eternal, uncreated, all-provident One. Jesus now makes claim to the same eternal being.

A further claim to His pre-fleshly eternal being is made in His prayer to the Father, when He said, "And now, Father, glorify thou me with thine own self with the glory which I had with thee before the world was" (17:5). He had glorified the Father through the work accomplished (v. 4); and now He seeks a return to that eternal glory which He had enjoyed with the Father "before the world was." He had not divested Himself of Deity when He became flesh, but had emptied Himself of the glory which had been His. It had been a voluntary surrender of heaven's glory that He might save men; and now He looked beyond the shame of the cross to the joy that was set before Him—the joy of the supreme act of love in fulfilling the complete will of God the Father in total unselfishness.

Omnipotence. While beyond Jordan on a preaching tour shortly before the time of His death, Jesus received word that His friend Lazarus of Bethany was sick. Jesus had claimed power to raise the dead and to give life (ch. 5); now an opportunity is presented to demonstrate that power. Jesus recognized the occasion as one in which He might be glorified in the sight of the people (11:4). Having waited two days until Lazarus was dead, and after discussing with the disciples the matter of returning to Bethany, Jesus said, "Our friend Lazarus is fallen asleep; but I go, that I may awake him out of sleep" (11:11). Here is the claim to divine power, the power to awaken one out of the sleep of death. The demonstration of the power will be considered later. At this

---

9. B. F. Westcott, *The Gospel According to John*, p. 140.

point only the claim to such power is presented. It was equivalent to a claim to omnipotence.

Omniscience. He lays claim not only to divine power but also to knowledge that transcends human knowledge. It was said of Him, "For he himself knew what was in man" (2:25). He knew the intimate life of the woman of Samaria; He knew of her husbands and present condition (4:16-18). He knew all about true worship (4:23, 24). He knew what He would do in the matter of feeding the five thousand (6:6); He knew what the multitude had in mind as they came to Him the next day (6:25, 26); He knew that it was Judas who would betray Him (6:70, 71). He knew the Jews sought to kill him (7:19). He knew all about God (7:29). He knew when His hour was come (12:23); He knew what kind of death He would die and what it would accomplish in the divine purpose (12:32, 33), As He ate the last supper with the disciples, He manifested a divine confidence that through death glory would result to Him and to His Father and that He would return to the Father. Everywhere, and at all times, Jesus manifested a knowledge superior to that of ordinary understanding. In Him was manifested the same omniscience that characterized His Father.

Omnipresence. The night before His death, as Jesus was preparing the disciples for His going away, He issued an imperative decree: "Believe in God, believe also in me" (14:1). This was followed with the assurance that in His Father's house were many abiding places, and that He was going to prepare a place for the faithful believers. This, no doubt, had reference to the way being opened into His Father's house by His death and resurrection. The Lord then promised that after having made preparation of a place for them, "I come again, and will receive you unto myself; that where I am there ye may be also" (14:3). It is doubtful if this coming of Jesus refers to the final coming at the end of the world or age. Instead, He assured them that after He had returned to the Father and completed the work of redemption for which He had come to earth, He would come to them here in their work. He would return to the Father and prepare a place for them that where He is the disciple might be also. This is to declare that He will be omnipresent—everywhere, with every one. But how is this to be accomplished?

Jesus' promise that the Holy Spirit would be sent to them is His own commentary on the promise to come and be with them.

"And I will pray the Father," He assured them, "and he shall give you another Comforter, that he may be with you for ever, even the Spirit of truth: whom the world cannot receive; for it beholdeth him not, neither knoweth him: ye know him; for he abideth with you, and shall be in you. *I will not leave you desolate: I come unto you*" (14:14-18). Here, in the same breath, Jesus promised them *another* Comforter, using the word *allos,* which means another of the same character or kind. The Spirit to come would be of the same character or kind as was He who was going away. In the same discourse He also said, "Ye heard how I said to you, I go away, and I come unto you" (v. 28). The coming of another of the same sort would fulfill the promise of Jesus; it would be the coming of Jesus in the person of the Holy Spirit. While present in the flesh He could be in only one place at a time; but in the Spirit He could be with each one all the time, and likewise with every disciple who should thereafter believe on Him. In this promise of omnipresence, He is claiming a divine attribute.

Even though He laid claim to deity and to divine attributes, while He was with the disciples He was human, a man as themselves, who could become tired and thirsty. On His journey from Judea to Galilee, Jesus "must needs pass through Samaria." When the group reached Jacob's well, the disciples left Him and went into the city to buy bread, but He, "being wearied with his journey, sat thus by the well" (4:6). And from the cross He made the simple statement, "I thirst" (19:28). He was a man with all the characteristics of man; yet He claimed the attributes of deity. The claims of Jesus in His relation to God are such that either He was and is the Son of God, or He was an impostor. He was not simply a good man.

His Relation to
the Messianic Hope

3

Before entering into a discussion of Jesus' claims relative to the messianic hope, it may be well to inquire briefly into the Old Testament background on which the Jewish expectation rested.

The Hebrew word for *messiah* and the Greek word for *christ* are both derived from words which mean "to anoint," and therefore they came to designate "an anointed one." Both priests and kings were anointed with oil when appointed to office. The word *anoint* is used as an adjective in the Old Covenant when referring to the office of priest: "the anointed priest" (Lev. 4:3, etc.). The word is used as a noun or title only when it refers to the king. For example, David spoke of Saul as "Jehovah's anointed" (I Sam. 24:6); David himself was later referred to by the same expression (II Sam. 19:21). In this way the word was used many times; but the word *messiah* is never used in the Old Covenant writings as a special title referring to the ideal or unique king of the future.

From the time of Jehovah's promise to David that of his descendants God would set one upon the throne and "establish the throne of his kingdom forever" (II Sam. 7:11-16), there developed in the divine revelation the idea of a unique or ideal king who was to come. As David drew near the time of his death, he described in his "last words" the character of the king that should rule over God's people: he should be "one that ruleth over men righteously, that ruleth in the fear of God." He should be "as the light of the morning, when the sun riseth, a morning without clouds," dispelling the clouds of darkness which had for so long engulfed the world. Further, among the ungodly, who should be as thorns to be thrust away, "because they cannot be taken with the hand," this ruler "must be armed with iron and the staff of a spear" that he might utterly burn them "in their place" (II Sam. 23:1-4, 6-7). He must possess that rare combination of the tenderness of the grass after the shower and the brightness of light when the clouds have been dispelled, combined with the toughness of iron.

No sooner had David said this than there was wrung from his lips the confession, "Verily my house is not so with God"; there were none among his children who could measure up to the standard. "Yet," he continues, "he hath made with me an everlasting covenant, ordered in all things, and sure: for it is all my salvation, and all my desire, although he maketh it not to grow" (*Ibid.*, v. 5); that is, it is not to be fulfilled immediately. David realized that he and the nation must look to a future seed whom Jehovah would anoint for the fulfilled desire of a king of such stature, one who would rule in righteousness (Ps. 45:6), yet rule among his enemies with a rod of iron (Pss. 2:9; 110:2).

It was not until the days of Isaiah that this doctrine of an ideal king, one related both to God and man, again blazed up as a clear and burning hope. As a sign, to the house of David one would be born of a virgin, whose name should be called "Immanuel (God with us)" (Isa. 7:13, 14). This child born, this son given, should be called "Mighty God," "Everlasting Father," "Prince of Peace," who should sit upon the throne of David, and upon his kingdom, "to establish it, and to uphold it with justice and with righteousness from henceforth even for ever." The zeal of Jehovah would perform this (Isa. 9:6-7). The ideal king is further described as being anointed with the Spirit of Jehovah, as judging in righteousness and with equity, and as smiting the earth "with the rod of his mouth" (Isa. 11:1-5). He would stand as an ensign, or rallying point, of the people and the nations who would seek him (v. 10).

Micah, a contemporary of Isaiah, prophesied that after the

travail of tribulation in Babylon there would be a return of the former dominion, the rule of David's house (Mic. 4:6-10). He who should rule would come out of Beth-lehem, the village of David, of the tribe of Judah, "whose goings forth are from of old, from everlasting" (Mic. 5:2); therefore, He would be an eternal one. He should feed His flock in the strength of Jehovah, and He would become great to the ends of the earth (v. 4).

About one hundred years after Isaiah and Micah, the prophet Jeremiah promised, "Behold, the days come, saith Jehovah, that I will raise unto David a righteous Branch, and he shall reign as king and deal wisely." Through Him Judah and Israel should be saved; He would be called, "Jehovah our righteousness" (Jer. 23:5, 6). Here is portrayed the Branch or Shoot of David to be raised as a savior-king, called "Jehovah our righteousness," that is, "he by whom Jehovah deals (distributes or aportions) righteousness."[1]

Ezekiel, who prophesied in Babylon while Jeremiah was in Judah, described the one to come as a shepherd-prince, feeding and caring for the people of God (Ezek. 34:23, 24). He should be a prince forever, ruling over a reunited people under an everlasting covenant (37:24-28).

Another hundred years later Zechariah identified the one to come as Jehovah's servant, "the Branch" (Zech. 3:8). This man, whose name is the Branch, would build the temple of Jehovah, bear the glory, "sit and rule upon his throne; and . . . be a priest upon his throne" (Zech. 6:12, 13). Here the one to come is identified as a king and a priest, sitting upon his throne and holding the twofold office. Further, he would be identified as a king, just and lowly, "bringing salvation," whose rule should be "from sea to sea, and from the River to the ends of the earth" (Zech. 9:9, 10). This again identifies Him as a savior-king.

The scope of this present volume forbids the introduction of other promises which are found in the writings of the Old Covenant and which point to the coming of an ideal and unique king, an anointed one, or Messiah, of the seed of David. He is described as ruling as king and priest upon His throne, related to God and to man, reigning and judging in righteousness, saving and delivering His people, feeding and caring for them as a shepherd, and cutting

---

1. Keil and Delitzsch, *Commentary on the Old Testament*, "Jeremiah," Vol. I, p. 353.

short His enemies with a rod of iron. During the period between
the covenants, the hope which grew out of these promises became
a very definite anticipation among the Jews. To be sure, erroneous ideas became intermingled with the true to the point that by
the time Jesus came the people of Israel held many distorted
concepts of what their Messiah should be; but the anticipation of a
savior-king, based on the promises of the prophets, was a strong
factor in their thinking. They expected Him to appear suddenly,
but when He should come, it would be from "no one knoweth
whence" (John 7:27); also, it seems that they were expecting Him
to perform signs, for the multitude asked, "When the Christ shall
come, will he do more signs than those which this man hath
done?" (7:31). From these Old Covenant promises we turn now to
the Gospel of John for the claims of Jesus in His relation to this
messianic hope of the prophets.

He Confessed Himself To Be the Messiah

After a visit to Jerusalem in the early part of His ministry, Jesus
returned to Galilee through Samaria. As He and His disciples came
to a city called Sychar, Jesus paused by Jacob's well to rest while
the disciples went into the city to buy necessary provisions. As He
was awaiting their return, a woman came out to the well to draw
water. Jesus opened the way to a serious conversation with her by
asking for a drink of water. As the conversation passed from a
drink of water to the woman's private life, then to the question of
Jesus' being a prophet, and finally to the question of worship and
its place and true character, the woman said, "I know that Messiah
cometh (he that is called Christ): when he is come, he will declare
unto us all things" (4:25). These words seem to reflect a deep
yearning of the woman's heart and to express a long-desired
expectation. The statement of the woman concerning the Messiah
gave Jesus the opportunity He sought and to which He had been
leading. He calmly and graciously made reply, "I that speak unto
thee am he" (v. 26). But even here He did not tell her that He was
the Messiah until He had brought her to the point of realizing the
spiritual nature of true religion.

Months later, when Jesus had gone up to Jerusalem to the feast
of dedication, the Jews gathered about Him and said, "How long
dost thou hold us in suspense? If thou art the Christ, tell us

plainly" (10:24). Was the question raised for the purpose of embroiling Jesus in further controversy with the Pharisees? If He should claim to be the Messiah, His claim would be so opposite to the Pharisaic concept of a Messiah that they would seek His destruction; or, do "the words seem to betray an unsatisfied longing which seeks rest, if it can be gained, even from this strange teacher?"[2] The discussion which followed seems to point to the former, for neither did He measure up to the expectation of the Jews or of the Pharisees, nor were they impressed by the evidence of the restoring of sight to the man born blind (ch. 9), which was in the background of the discussion.

Jesus did not answer directly, as He had responded to the woman in Samaria, but replied, "I told you, and ye believe not: the works that I do in my Father's name, these bear witness of me" (v. 25). At no time prior had He told them in so many words that He was the Christ. He could not, for they were not prepared for a Messiah such as Jesus offered them in Himself. His teaching bore witness that He was the Messiah; the works which He had done in the Father's name had testified to the same; earlier He had told them plainly, "Your father Abraham rejoiced to see my day; and he saw it, and was glad. . . . Verily, verily, I say unto you, Before Abraham was born, I am" (8:56, 58). These should have made the request of the Jews unnecessary, but they did not. The centuries intervening between the promises of the prophets and the coming of Jesus had given rise to the expectation of a political Messiah who would deliver them from the bondage to Rome and restore the political kingdom of united Israel. With this thought so deeply burned into their minds, the Jews were blind to the evidence Jesus was offering them in His life, teaching, and works to support the idea that He was the Messiah of promise.

He Acknowledged Himself To Be King

The Jews were correct in their understanding that the Messiah should be a king; but they were mistaken in their understanding of the nature of the king that had been promised. After Jesus had fed the multitude of five thousand men with five barley loaves and two small fishes, the Jews were so impressed with Him as the kind

---

2. Westcott, p. 157.

of Messiah for which they had been looking that they were ready to crown Him king. Under such a king there would be no need for a large commissariat department in their army; one person would be able to carry enough provisions for the whole military force. Besides, with such a king they could not be defeated; for if He could perform this miracle He could perform others. Their determination was detected by Jesus, for John says, "Jesus therefore perceiving that they were about to come and take him by force, to make him king, withdrew again into the mountain himself alone" (6:15).

This incident led to the sermon preached the next day on "the bread of life." Jesus was determined to put them to the test to see if they would accept a spiritual Messiah; the discourse on the bread of life was that test. A. T. Robertson calls this chapter in Jesus' ministry "The Sifting of the People";[3] and truly, it was just that. The sermon sifted them down to a handful, for following the discourse, "many of his disciples went back, and walked no more with him" (6:66). They could not accept a spiritual king. Like their fathers who in the days of Samuel had asked for a king to judge them and go out before them and fight their battles (I Sam. 8:19-20), these demanded a political leader who would deliver them from the yoke of Rome. When Jesus rejected their political crown, He bargained for a crown of thorns and for a cross as His bier.

Months later, as Jesus came to Jerusalem to the Passover, a great multitude having heard that He was in Bethany and was coming to the feast, "took the branches of the palm trees, and went forth to meet him, and cried out, Hosanna: Blessed is he that cometh in the name of the Lord, even the King of Israel" (12:12-13). The quotation is from Psalm 118:25, 26; the word *Hosanna* "is the Grecized form" of the Hebrew which means, "Save, I pray!"[4] The cry is for salvation by Him who is now coming in the name of the Lord (Jehovah) in keeping with God's promise of old. They anticipated His being crowned King of Israel in fulfillment of the promise of God that a king of the seed of David should sit on David's throne. It is their cry of acknowledgment that Jesus is the Messiah-king. Jesus acknowledged the token of recognition on their part by finding a young ass on which to ride as He entered

3. A. T. Robertson, *The Divinity of Christ*, pp. 73-75.

4. H. R. Reynolds, *Pulpit Commentary*, "John," Vol. II, p. 135.

the city, thereby fulfilling the prediction of Zechariah, who had so vividly foretold the event as a part of the messianic expectation (Zech. 9:9-10). In accepting their homage, Jesus was acknowledging Himself to be the messianic Savior-king of Old Testament prophecy.

It was not, however, until He was before Pilate a few days later that Jesus acknowledged in so many words that He was the King of Jewish expectation. Forced against his will to take the case and try Jesus, Pilate asked Him, "Art thou the King of the Jews?" (18:33). Although His omniscience could have provided Him with the desired information, Jesus' reply may indicate that He had not heard the charge made against Him in Pilate's presence (v. 34). However, the question was one that could not have been answered "yes" or "no." Jesus therefore would have Pilate tell Him whether the question was from Pilate, a Roman and asked from the Roman point of view, or from the Jews and asked from the Jewish point of view. From the strictly political Roman point of view, the answer would be "no." From what should have been the Jewish viewpoint, it would be "yes." The governor's contemptuous reply indicates a total ignorance of the matter. With this point cleared up, Jesus was ready to answer Pilate's second question, "What hast thou done?" The answer was forthright, "My kingdom is not of this world: if my kingdom were of this world, then would my servants fight, that I should not be delivered to the Jews: but now is my kingdom not from hence" (v. 36). This presents a clear distinction between the kingdom of Pilate and the kingdom of Jesus. One is of this world, political in its nature; the other is not of this world and is spiritual in its nature. Again Pilate asked the question, "Art thou a king then?" to which Jesus made the simple answer, "Thou sayest that I am king (marginal reading, 'Thou sayest it, because I am a king')" (v. 37). Jesus again declared the nature of His kingdom over which He is King when He said that He came to bear witness to the truth. His kingdom is a kingdom of truth, a spiritual kingdom, over which He reigns as a spiritual King. This is the nature of King and kingdom foretold by the prophets of the Old Covenant; the Jews should have been prepared for it.

He Claimed To Speak from God—Therefore To Be a Prophet

The questions asked by the deputation of priests and Levites sent from the Pharisees to John the Baptist imply that the Jews

were looking for three persons to appear: the Christ, Elijah, and
"the prophet." Their expectation of a Messiah has been dealt with
previously. The expectation of the return of Elijah rested on the
promise of Malachi 4, and the expectation of a special prophet,
apart from the Messiah, was based on the words of Moses in
Deuteronomy 18.

In answer to their question, "Who art thou?", the Baptist
replied, "I am not the Christ." They were not yet satisfied but
countered with two additional questions, "What then? Art thou
Elijah? And he saith, I am not. Art thou the prophet? And he
answered, No" (1:19-22). Their final question further confirms the conclusion that they were expecting three persons to
appear, as they asked, "Why then baptizest thou, if thou art not
the Christ, neither Elijah, neither the prophet?" (v. 25). Although
they looked for three persons, the fulfillment of their hope was
being realized in one.

The idea of a Messiah and a prophet was not peculiar to the
Jerusalem Jews, but prevailed among the Jews in general. When
Jesus was in Jerusalem for the feast of tabernacles and had invited
all who thirsted to come to Him and drink, He promised that from
within those who should come to Him there would flow rivers of
living water. Immediately there arose a division among the multitude as to who He was. Upon hearing these words from Jesus,
some said, "This is of a truth the prophet. Others said, This is the
Christ. But some said, What, doth the Christ come out of Galilee?"
(7:40ff.). This division that arose among them over Jesus makes it
clear that they were expecting the appearance of both a Messiah
and a prophet.

However, among others there seems to have been the idea that
the prophet and the Messiah would be the same. In Galilee, after
Jesus had fed the multitude with the five barley loaves and two
fishes, the people were so impressed with the sign that they said,
"This is of a truth the prophet that cometh into the world. Jesus
therefore perceiving that they were about to come and take him
by force, to make him king, withdrew" (6:14, 15). Jesus is here
identified in the thinking of the Galileans as the prophet and king;
He is the prophet whom they would crown king. The two are
identified by the people as one.

Moses, in his farewell address to the people, warned Israel that
when they should come into the land that God would give them

they were not to follow the practice of the nations in seeking supernatural information. They should not suffer a diviner, an enchanter, a sorcerer, a charmer, one who used divination, a consulter with a familiar spirit, a wizard, or a necromancer to live; neither should they appeal to them, for upon these the nations depended. Instead, when God should desire to give them special information, He would raise up a prophet from among them through whom He would speak. God had already defined a prophet as "a mouth," one who speaks for another (Exod. 4:16; 7:1). Wherefore He now said to Moses, "I will raise them up a prophet from among their brethren, like unto thee; and I will put my words in his mouth, and he shall speak unto them all that I shall command him. And it shall come to pass, that whosoever will not hearken unto my words which he shall speak in my name, I will require it of him" (Deut. 18:18, 19). This points clearly to the fact that a prophet of Jehovah was to be one in whose mouth God would put His words and that He would require everyone to give heed to that word as His word. The prophecy also infers that there would be at some time a special prophet, a lawgiver, like Moses. It was on the ground of this statement that the Jews looked for a special prophet to come, one who in a particular way would fulfill the ideal. The idea of a peculiar Redeemer-prophet, in whose mouth Jehovah would put His words, was further and more fully advanced by Isaiah when he said, "And a Redeemer will come to Zion, and unto them that turn from transgression in Jacob, saith Jehovah. And as for me, this is my covenant with them, saith Jehovah: my Spirit that is upon thee, and my words which I have put in thy mouth, shall not depart out of thy mouth, nor out of the mouth of thy seed, nor out of the mouth of thy seed's seed, saith Jehovah, from henceforth and for ever" (Isa. 59:20, 21). The word *Redeemer* identifies the one to come as Savior, whom God identifies as a prophet by putting His words in the mouth of the Redeemer.

When the Samaritan woman said to Jesus, "Sir, I perceive that thou art a prophet" (4:19), He neither denied the implication nor corrected her. In fact, He "himself testified that a prophet hath no honor in his own country" (4:43ff.), applying the proverb to Himself. In all His teaching Jesus claimed no originality for what He taught, but He claimed that the words which He spoke were from God, that God gave them to Him. In this He claimed to be a

prophet, for He was claiming all the traits of a true prophet as God
had promised through Moses; namely, that he should speak the
words that God would put in his mouth.

In reference to His being a prophet, consider the claims of Jesus
as He repeatedly asserted that both His actions and His words were
directed by His Father. Of His actions He said, "The Son can do
nothing of himself, but what he seeth the Father doing: for what
things soever he doeth, these the Son also doeth in like manner"
(5:19); "For I am come down from heaven, not to do mine own
will, but the will of him that sent me" (6:38); "And as the Father
gave me commandment, even so I do" (14:31). He was doing only
what the Father gave Him to do.

Jesus was even more particular in emphasizing that in His
teaching He was directed by the Father, as He said, "My teaching
is not mine, but his that sent me" (7:16); "And the things which I
heard from him, these speak I unto the world" (8:26); "As the
Father taught me, I speak these things" (8:28); "For I spake not
from myself; but the Father that sent me, he hath given me a
commandment, what I should say, and what I should speak. And I
know that his commandment is life eternal: the things therefore
which I speak, even as the Father hath said unto me, so I speak"
(12:49ff.); "The words that I say unto you I speak not from
myself: but the Father abiding in me doeth his works" (14:10);
"And the word which ye hear is not mine, but the Father's who
sent me" (14:24); and finally, "For all things that I heard from
my Father I have made known unto you" (15:15). In claiming
that He spoke only that which God gave Him to speak, He was
claiming to be a true prophet of God—the prophet like unto
Moses.

In these claims made by Jesus, He implied that in Him was the
final revelation of God and of His will to man. In His prayer to the
Father, He said, "And this is life eternal, that they should know
thee the only true God, and him whom thou didst send, even Jesus
Christ" (17:3). If life eternal is to be conditioned on knowing
God, then God must have revealed Himself completely. Jesus'
mission was to reveal God. He claimed that to know Him is to
know the Father, to see Him is to see the Father, and to hear Him
is to hear the Father (14:9ff.). In this same prayer (ch. 17), He
continued, "I glorified thee on the earth, having accomplished the
work which thou hast given me to do" (17:4). If Jesus had

revealed the Father and His will and His way so that man could know God, then that revelation of God must be complete; and if complete, then final, for there could be no revelation beyond that which is complete and full. Jesus, therefore, by implication claims to be *the* Prophet who should come.

He Claimed To Be the "Good Shepherd"—A Messianic Hope

One of Jesus' claims so often overlooked as a claim to the messianic expectation is the reference to Himself as the "good shepherd." The discourse on Himself as the shepherd followed the restoring of sight to the man born blind and Jesus' brush with the Pharisees (ch. 9). Jesus here uses an allegory of a shepherd and his flock; this was familiar to all His hearers. But His claim to be the good shepherd is more than an allegory used to teach an immediate lesson. The claim identified Him with the Old Testament prophecies which pointed to a shepherd-king who was to come. If Jesus measures up to the promises made by the prophets, He is thereby proved to be the Messiah of prophecy and the fulfillment of Israel's hope.

Jesus spoke of "thieves and robbers" who came before Him; these were men who had come to steal and to destroy. Evidently He was referring to false shepherds who had preceded His coming. He proceeds with the claim, "I am the good shepherd: the good shepherd layeth down his life for the sheep" (10:11). In contrasting Himself with the hirelings who flee when danger appears, He further says, "I am the good shepherd; and I know mine own, and mine own know me . . . And other sheep I have, which are not of this fold: them also I must bring, and they shall hear my voice; and they shall become one flock, one shepherd" (vv. 14, 16). And finally, He claimed that "no one taketh it (my life) away from me, but I lay it down of myself. I have power to lay it down, and I have power to take it again. This commandment received I from my Father" (v. 18).

In these claims Jesus was identifying Himself with the messianic promises of old. A few of these are here introduced to show the relation between what Jesus said of Himself and what the prophets had said of the shepherd who would come. Isaiah, the great prophet of hope, comforted the people who would be captives in

Babylon with the assurance that good tidings of God's presence in their midst would be proclaimed to them. The Lord Jehovah would be in their midst as a mighty one, ruling and rewarding His saints; and "He will feed his flock like a shepherd, he will gather the lambs in his arm, and carry them in his bosom, and will gently lead those that have their young" (Isa. 40:11). This was to be the assurance and comfort of the exiles; Jehovah would be their shepherd.

Ezekiel, the prophet to the people of the captivity in Babylon, sees the fulfillment of Isaiah's prophecy in Jehovah as the shepherd of the people in this foreign land. In glowing words Ezekiel portrays Jehovah as searching out His people in and beyond the captivity and bringing them back, Himself being their shepherd and judge. But this picture blends into the messianic hope as Jehovah looks beyond the time of His own shepherding of the sheep to that time when He would care for them through David, His shepherd. "For thus saith the Lord Jehovah: Behold, I myself, even I, will search for my sheep, and will seek them out . . . I myself will be the shepherd of my sheep, and I will cause them to lie down . . . Behold, I judge between sheep and sheep, the rams and the he-goats . . . And I will set up one shepherd over them, and he shall feed them, even my servant David; he shall feed them, and he shall be their shepherd. And I, Jehovah, will be their God, and my servant David prince among them . . . And ye my sheep, the sheep of my pasture, are men, and I am your God, saith the Lord Jehovah" (Ezek. 34:11-31). In this prophecy Jehovah is portrayed as shepherd over His people as He brings them back from the Babylonian captivity, caring for and judging them. But from this He looks to that time when through David, the "prince-shepherd," He would shepherd them as their God. Jesus claimed to be the good shepherd. He claimed that it was the Father in Him doing His works. Therefore it was God in Christ, judging and gathering, feeding and shepherding His sheep.

But Ezekiel was not finished. Jehovah told him to take two sticks and write upon one, "For Judah," and upon the other, "For Joseph, the stick of Ephraim, and for all the house of Israel his companions." The prophet was to join the two sticks together in his hand. By this act God was promising that He would gather both those of Judah and of Israel who were scattered at that time and make of them not two but one nation; "so shall they be my people, and I will be their God." From this uniting of the two upon their return from captivity, the Lord looked into the future, passing over the intervening years, to the coming of Messiah. He continues, "And my servant David shall be king over them; and they all shall have one shepherd . . . and David my servant shall be their prince for ever." God then promised that He would make with them a covenant of peace, an everlasting covenant, and that He would set His sanctuary in their midst forevermore. "My tabernacle also shall be with them; and I will be their God, and they shall be my people" (Ezek. 37:15-28). Jesus, the descendant of David, must surely have had these prophecies in mind as He spoke of Himself as the "good shepherd," laying down His life for the sheep and gathering them into one fold as they would hear His voice and follow Him. In Him the shepherd-prince-covenant promises were being fulfilled.

The prophet Zechariah presented a vivid contrast between the false shepherds and the good shepherd. Because of the lies of the false shepherds, the prophet said of the people, "Therefore they go their way like sheep, they are afflicted, because there is no shepherd. Mine anger is kindled against the shepherds (the false shepherds), and I will punish the he-goats (the leaders); for Jehovah of hosts hath visited his flock, the house of Judah, and will make them as his goodly horse in the battle" (Zech. 10:2, 3). He hears "a voice of the wailing of the shepherds! for their glory is destroyed" (Zech. 11:3). As a further contrast, Jehovah presents the false and the true as He cuts off three false shepherds, "for my soul was weary of them, and their soul also loathed me." The good shepherd was then sold for thirty pieces of silver; in that day the covenant that God had made with the two nations was broken and the brotherhood between Judah and Israel was dissolved (Zech. 11:4-14). This indicates that when the good shepherd would be sold for thirty pieces of silver, the old order, the covenant of the fleshly brotherhood, would pass away. With its passing Jesus would gather into one flock both Jews and Gentiles.

One final word from Zechariah will suffice concerning the Messiah-shepherd prophecies. Jehovah promised that a fountain would be "opened to the house of David and to the inhabitants of Jerusalem, for sin and for uncleanness" (Zech. 13:1). In close relation to this event, the prophet said, "Awake, O sword, against my shepherd, and against the man that is my fellow, saith Jehovah of hosts: smite the shepherd, and the sheep shall be scattered" (Zech. 13:7). Here is declared the relation of the shepherd to Jehovah as "my fellow," that is, one of the same nature, sharing a community of nature with God. In laying down His life that He might take it up again, Jesus fulfilled this prophecy that the shepherd would be put to death; He received this commandment from His Father (John 10:18). The sheep were scattered, that they might be brought together again in one fold, under the one shepherd, receiving a fuller and more abundant life (John 10:10, 11, 16-18).

These prophecies pointed to the coming of a shepherd-king, a Savior, one related to Jehovah, whose life would be laid down for the sheep that He might gather them together into one fold. Jesus claimed to be that shepherd, fulfilling the promise of God and the hope of the Old Covenant prophets.

He Confessed Himself To Be the Son of God

The Messiah of Old Testament hope was definitely related to God as His Son. Others were called "sons of God," but the King of promise should be the Son of God in a special sense. When Jehovah promised David that He would raise up one of his seed to sit upon his throne, He said, "I will be his father, and he shall be my son" (II Sam. 7:14). The prophecy included Solomon, but it looked beyond him, as is indicated by the psalm of Ethan which dealt with the covenant Jehovah made with David. Here it is said, "He shall cry unto me, Thou art my Father . . . I also will make him my first-born, the highest of the kings of the earth" (Ps. 89:26, 27). Further, in the second psalm, wherein is described a general uprising of the nations against Jehovah, it is said that the rulers took counsel together "against Jehovah, and against his anointed (Messiah)" (Ps. 2:2). In spite of this general uprising against Jehovah and His Messiah (anointed one), God said, "Yet I have set my king upon my holy hill of Zion" (v. 6). The anointed one then speaks, saying, "I will tell of the decree: Jehovah said unto me, Thou art my son; This day have I begotten thee" (v. 7). Clearly, the Messiah-king should be not only of the seed of David but also the Son of God in a special sense. The word *anointed*, as so used in the psalm, is not used as a title but simply to imply one anointed to fill the office as king.

Jesus claimed for Himself a relation to God different from that of others—a relation that definitely fulfilled this hope of prophecy. He summarized this clear recognition of difference when He said, "Touch me not; for I am not yet ascended unto the Father." There was but one Father of both Himself and His brethren; but the relation of the two to the Father was different. This difference was emphasized as He continued, "But go unto my brethren, and say to them, I ascend unto *my* Father and *your* Father, and *my* God and *your* God" (20:17). This difference in relation to the Father is maintained throughout all of Jesus' teaching; never does He identify Himself with them in relation to the Father by saying, "Our Father." When Jesus taught the disciples to pray, saying, "Our Father" (Matt. 6:9), He did not include Himself but taught them to recognize a common brotherhood among themselves and a common Fatherhood of God to themselves.

Jesus often referred to Himself as "the Son" in such a relation to "the Father" that the hearer could not help understanding that He was speaking of God and of His special relation to Him as the Son of God. Having healed a lame man in Jerusalem, Jesus brought upon Himself the wrath of the Jews because He "did these things upon the sabbath." In His defense of what He had done, Jesus said, "My Father worketh even until now, and I work" (5:17). This so angered the Jews that they sought to kill Him, for not only had He broken the sabbath, as they insisted, "but also called God his own Father, making himself equal with God" (5:18). This incident, the claim on Jesus' part, and the charge by the Jews led to a series of further bold claims by Jesus for the special Son and Father relation which He affirmed existed. "The Son," said He, "can do nothing of himself, but what he seeth the Father doing: for what things soever he doeth, these the Son also doeth in like manner" (5:19). He proceeded in His Father-Son relation by claiming equality with God in raising the dead and giving them life (v. 21), in judging, as the Father had given all judgment to the Son (v. 22), and in His sharing equal honor with the Father, charging that to fail to honor the Son is to withhold honor from the Father (v. 23).

Jesus further identified Himself as the Son of God when He said, "The hour cometh, and now is, when the dead shall hear the voice of the Son of God; and they that hear shall live" (v. 25), for both the Father and the Son have life within themselves (v. 26). The climax to a recognition of this Father-Son relationship was reached in His prayer to the Father immediately before His death when He said, "Father, the hour is come; glorify thy Son, that the Son may glorify thee . . . I glorified thee on the earth . . . And now, Father, glorify thou me with thine own self with the glory which I had with thee before the world was" (17:1-5). "The Son" is Jesus, "the Father" is God; the relation sustained is one of a unique nature, a relationship that extends back to "before the world was," which makes Jesus different from all men.

It is not certain whether Jesus Himself spoke the words found in 3:16, or whether these words are the explanation by John; scholars consulted are divided about evenly on the subject. If Jesus spoke them, then He here declared Himself to be the "only begotten Son" of God. In their relation to the context, the words seem to be a continuation of His discussion with Nicodemus, and therefore His own words. If, however, these are the words of John the apostle, there are numerous occasions other than this where He confessed Himself clearly to be the Son of God.

After having had his sight restored by Jesus, the man born blind defended his benefactor as a prophet (9:17), and later as one who came from God, else "he could do nothing" (v. 33). The Pharisees, being angered at the man's obstinate defense of Jesus, "cast him out" of their meeting and from any fellowship with them or the synagogue. When Jesus heard that they had cast him out, He found the man formerly blind and asked, "Dost thou believe on the Son of God?" Puzzled at the question, the man asked, "And who is he, Lord, that I may believe on him?" To this question Jesus made answer, "Thou hast both seen him, and he it is that speaketh with thee" (9:33-37). In this reply Jesus made a clear and positive claim to being the Son of God.

Probably the supreme act on Jesus' part in relating Himself to the Messiah and in confessing Himself to be the Son of God was His acceptance of worship from the man whom He had healed. Having confessed his faith in Jesus, that He was the Son of God, it is said, "And he worshipped him" (9:38). Jesus had taught that God is the object of worship and that He must be worshipped in spirit and truth (4:23, 24). Not only had Jesus allowed the man to believe that He was the Son of God, but also He now allowed him to demonstrate his faith by worshiping Him. When Jesus thus accepted the worship of this man without correcting him, He placed Himself either in the position of acknowledging Himself to be God, that is Deity, or in the unenviable position of being both a blasphemer and a hypocrite of supreme rank.

Not only did Jesus confess Himself to be the Son of God and accept worship as God, but also He accepted the same confession from others without any correction of their statement. After the discourse on the bread of life, when many of His disciples turned back, Jesus asked the disciples if they also would go away; whereupon Peter replied by asking, "To whom shall we go? thou hast the words of eternal life. And we have believed and know that thou art the Holy One of God" (6:66-69). Jesus made no effort to correct the thought in Peter's mind.

A more direct confession was made by Martha when she met Jesus as He came to console her and her sister over the death of their brother. When confronted with His claim, "I am the resurrection, and the life," she replied, "Yea, Lord: I have believed that thou art the Christ, the Son of God" (11:25ff.). Here the Messiahship of Jesus is connected with His Sonship of God. He denied neither, but recognized both. His claim to the title "Son of God" was tantamount to His recognition of Himself as the Messiah. There can be no doubt that He both confessed Himself to be the Son of God and allowed others likewise to confess Him as the Son of God, both of these in relation to the messianic hope. The record speaks for itself.

He Identified Himself as "the Son of Man"

Jesus preferred and used the designation "Son of man" over that of any other title or salutation by which He was recognized. As a designation of Himself, Jesus alone used the expression; no other used it of Him in the Gospels except when certain Jews asked, in response to a statement He had made concerning Himself, "How sayest thou, The Son of man must be lifted up? who is this Son of man?" (12:34). In all the writings which followed the Gospels, the designation is used only by Stephen, who, as he was being stoned, looked up and saw Jesus standing by the right hand of God (Acts 7:56). Commenting on the use of the title by Stephen, Westcott says, "As 'the Son of man' He is revealed to the eyes of His first martyr, that Christians may learn that that which

is begun in weakness shall be completed in eternal majesty."[5] The
expression "like a son of man" is used of Jesus by John in the
Book of Revelation (Rev. 1:13; 14:14). Some have suggested that
in these two statements John has in mind Daniel 7:13ff. This is
quite possible, since the one walking among the lampstands and
coming on a cloud in judgment is the one who ascended on clouds
to the ancient of days and there received the kingdom, dominion,
and glory.

There is little or no doubt that in the use of this title Jesus
identified Himself with humanity, "in whom the complete concep-
tion of manhood was absolutely attained," and in whom all that
belongs to every man of every race of every age was summed up. It
is without doubt that the idea of the true humanity of Christ lies
at the foundation of the title. For various reasons Jesus may have
adopted this title as peculiar to Himself. Vos seems to have well
summed up the matter when he says that the "reason lay in the
fact that the title Son of man stood farthest removed from every
possible Jewish prostitution of the Messianic office."[6] Jesus never
used the title "Messiah" when speaking of Himself, though when
asked by others He confessed Himself to have been the Messiah.
Many think of the title "Son of man" primarily as it relates Jesus
to humanity and as it emphasizes His human nature. But a consideration of the context in which the title is used in the Gospels,
especially of John, points clearly to its use as a messianic title as
well.

Before considering Jesus' use of the term "Son of man" and His
claims associated with it as found in the Fourth Gospel, it may
prove profitable to pay attention to one of the strongly messianic
passages in Daniel. The prophet relates his vision of the four beasts
coming up out of the sea, each terrible in its aspect (Dan. 7:1-8),
and explains that they are four kingdoms. The seer then beheld
thrones placed, with "one who was ancient of days" sitting on one
of them (Dan. 7:9). This was a judgment scene in which the "little
horn" and the fourth beast were judged and slain. Daniel then
says, "I saw in the night-visions, and, behold, there came with
the clouds of heaven one like unto a *son of man,* and he came even
to the ancient of days, and they brought him near before him.
And there was given him dominion, and glory, and a kingdom,

---

5. Westcott, p. 35.
6. Geerhardus Vos, *The Self-Disclosure of Jesus,* p. 254.

that all peoples, nations, and languages should serve him: his dominion is an everlasting dominion, which shall not pass away, and his kingdom that which shall not be destroyed" (Dan. 7:13, 14). Most scholars admit that this is a messianic prophecy, with the messianic kingdom in view. The "ancient of days" in the vision clearly signifies God. His throne is in heaven, hence it is a vision from heaven's point of view presenting the coming of one like unto a son of man from earth to heaven, where he receives dominion and glory and a kingdom from the hand of "one who was ancient of days."

The question is now raised as to who is this one "like unto a son of man." In what sense does the seer use the expression, as a title or to relate this one to humanity? Inasmuch as Daniel here presents the messianic kingdom, it follows that there can be no such kingdom without an anointed one to reign over it; hence the one "like unto a son of man," to whom is given the dominion and glory and kingdom must be the Messiah. Although this is a messianic prophecy and presents the Messiah as "like unto a son of man," it seems evident that the term as here used is not parallel to Jesus' use of it; the one in Daniel's vision is not called "*the* son of man." Jesus' use of the expression as a title is new; it is peculiar to Himself alone. In the vision Daniel sees one like unto a son of man come to the throne of God from whom he receives the kingship; he is one who has qualified himself to take the reins of government and rule over the divine kingdom.

Some think that Daniel used the expression "like unto a son of man" in a collective sense to represent spiritual Israel. The contention is based on the verses that follow, in which it is said that "the saints of the Most High shall receive the kingdom, and possess the kingdom for ever, even for ever and ever" (Dan. 7:18; see also vv. 21, 27). It is true that the expression "son of man" is used collectively or representatively in some places, for example, Psalm 8:4-8, quoted in Hebrews 2:6, 7. But Daniel uses it simply as descriptive of the human appearance of the being whom he saw in the vision; he had the qualities and characteristics of a man and was one who had proved himself worthy of the kingdom given to him. In the vision which followed the saints were given the kingdom by the Son of Man to whom it had been given.

In His use of the words "Son of man" as a title, Jesus identified Himself with the messianic hope of the past, with the needs of the

present, and with the judgment of the future. This is realized from
a consideration of the language of Jesus as recorded in the Gospel
of John. His words to Nathanael, "Ye shall see the heaven opened,
and the angels of God ascending and descending upon the Son of
man" (1:51), will be discussed in the following section. To Nicodemus He said, "And no one hath ascended into heaven, but he
that descended out of heaven, even the Son of man, who is in
heaven" (3:13). The expression "who is in heaven" is considered
by many as parenthetical. By this Jesus claimed for Himself the
distinction of being the heavenly man who had come from heaven,
combining within Himself as "Son of man" all that God would
have man to be, and one who, as man, is the hope of man.

In the next verse, as the Son of man, Jesus identifies Himself
with the sacrifice of one who would procure eternal life for the
lost: "And as Moses lifted up the serpent in the wilderness, even so
must the Son of man be lifted up; that whosoever believeth may in
him have eternal life" (3:14ff.). In being lifted up as a sacrifice in
humiliation, He identified Himself as the Suffering Servant of
messianic prophecy and hope. This is further attested when He
said, "When ye have lifted up the Son of man, then shall ye know
that I am he" (8:28). The claim "I am he" refers back to the claim
made for Himself in contrast to those whom He addressed, "Ye
are from beneath; I am from above: ye are of this world; I am not
of this world" (v. 23). The lifting up of Jesus would confirm His
claim to have been not of this world, but from above. The
confirmation would be established in the resurrection following
the lifting up, or crucifixion. Then finally, "The hour is come, that
the Son of man should be glorified . . . And I, if I be lifted up
from the earth, will draw all men unto myself" (12:23, 32). Here
the Son of man is being lifted up that He might draw all men unto
Himself. The "all men" included the Gentiles, at whose request to
see Jesus this statement had been elicited. The Jews did not
understand, so they responded with the question, "How sayest
thou, The Son of man must be lifted up? who is this Son of man?"
(v. 34).

The relation of Christ to the Suffering Servant of Isaiah will be
dealt with later; at the present let it suffice to point out that Jesus'
use of the title "Son of man" in these passages definitely was with
a messianic connotation. Isaiah, the great prophet of the Suffering
Servant, had said that the Spirit of Jehovah would be upon His

servant and that he would bring forth justice to the Gentiles (Isa. 42:1-4). Jesus said that the Son of man was being lifted up and that He would draw *all* men unto Himself. Isaiah declared further that the destiny of the Servant was that he should be exalted and lifted up, "and shall be very high" (Isa. 52:13). But before this exaltation, before He "should be glorified," He would be "despised, and rejected of men; a man of sorrows, and acquainted with grief: and as one from whom men hide their face" and esteem Him not (Isa. 53:3). By His humiliation this righteous servant should "justify many; and he shall bear their iniquities" (Isa. 53:11). As the Son of man lifted up, Jesus was identifying Himself with the humiliation of the one in whom should be salvation through His being lifted up.

Jesus also claimed that as the "Son of man" He provided the food and drink unto eternal life, a bread which had come down from heaven and which must be eaten in order to the possessing and maintaining of eternal life (6:27, 53).

Because He was related to man as "a son of man," God gave Him authority to execute judgment (5:27). However, the fact that the definite article is here omitted should not be pressed too strongly in defense of the human relationship, because the context strongly affirms the divine prerogatives of Jesus. This right to judge pertained to the present as well as the future and was related to the messianic expectation. Isaiah had said of the Branch that should come out of the stock of Jesse, "His delight shall be in the fear of Jehovah; and he shall not judge after the sight of his eyes, neither decide after the hearing of his ears; but with righteousness shall he judge the poor, and decide with equity for the meek of the earth; and he shall smite the earth with the rod of his mouth; and with the breath of his lips shall he slay the wicked" (Isa. 11:3, 4).

The title "Son of man" was not used by Jesus after His resurrection. The last time He so referred to Himself was as He and the disciples were eating the paschal supper together; He said, "Now is the Son of man glorified, and God is glorified in him; and God shall glorify him in himself, and straightway shall he glorify him" (13:31). The time was approaching when they "should behold the Son of man ascending where he was before" (6:62).

Jesus' use of the title "Son of man," as related to the messianic hope, may be summarized as follows: As Son of man (1:51) He

fulfills the promise of the "seed"; He is no earthly being, but is
from above and returns to the place where He was (3:13; 6:62);
He fulfills the expectation of a savior, and thereby identifies
Himself with the Suffering Servant (3:14; 8:28; 12:34); He has
authority to execute judgment (5:27); He provides eternal life for
men (6:27, 53); and when His work should have been completed,
He would enter into His glory (12:23; 13:31). He was the repre-
sentative of the whole race, the summing up of all that God would
provide for man and develop in man. He was *the* Son of man; in
His claims to such a title, He was identifying Himself as the
Messiah.

He Made Himself Known
as the Mediator
Between God and Man
—Man and God

In the beginning of His ministry when Nathanael acknowledged
Him as "the Son of God . . . the King of Israel" (1:49), Jesus
responded by saying to the group, "Verily, verily, I say unto you,
Ye shall see the heaven opened, and the angels of God ascending
and descending upon the Son of man" (v. 51). Jesus did not deny,
but rather acknowledged, the titles by which Nathanael recognized
Him and then chose for Himself the title "Son of man." Heaven,
through Him, the Son of man, was now opened, not to be closed
again. In Him was now fulfilled the dream of Jacob, the patriarch,
who "dreamed; and, behold, a ladder set up on the earth, and the
top of it reached to heaven; and, behold, the angels of God ascending and descending on it" (Gen. 28:12). Then followed the land
promise to Jacob, followed by the promise of universal blessing,
"And in thy seed shall all the families of the earth be blessed"
(v. 14).

In this reply to Nathanael's confession, Jesus made claim that in
Himself, the Son of man, from henceforth the messages from
heaven to earth and from earth to heaven would be communi-
cated. In this Jesus represented Himself as the Mediator between
God and man, and between man and God. In thus relating Himself
to the dream of Jacob, He also recognized Himself to be the
"seed" through which all the families of the earth should be
blessed. All men would be blessed in the communication from
God through Him, and through Him all would have the privilege of
communicating with the Father.

The claim that He was to be the medium of communication from heaven to earth and from earth to heaven introduced Jesus as the Mediator of salvation, the one sent that men might not perish but have eternal life (3:16-18), and the revealer of light from God to man (3:19-21). He came from heaven to reveal the Father's will (6:38), which men could recognize as being from God if they desired to do His will (7:16, 17). He was the Lord and Teacher, the teacher sent from God (13:13, 14) to reveal God and, when lifted up, to draw men to God (12:32). In all this He was the Mediator between God and man, the "ladder" over whom should come the message of God to the human family.

But more, He was the one through whom man should come to the Father and the one through whom the message of man should be brought to the Eternal One. Jesus' claim was, "I am the way, and the truth, and the life: no one cometh unto the Father, but by me" (14:6). He claimed that He is "the door" and that through Him men would find access to the spiritual pasture and to divine protection (10:9). He further promised that He would go and prepare a place for the disciples, that where He is there they should be also (14:2, 3). Further, men should ask through His name (14:14) and all petitions should be made to the Father through Him (15:16; 16:23-24). The longest recorded prayer made by Jesus to the Father is that of an intercessory nature as He presented to the Father an account of His own work, presented a petition for the apostles who should carry on that work in His stead, and concluded with a special prayer for the disciples who should believe on Him through their preaching (ch. 17).

The door to heaven is now open; Jesus, the Son of man, is the one on whom the angels will ascend and descend from henceforth. As such He is the one Mediator between God and man and between man and God. He is the fulfillment of Jacob's dream and the promise made by God to him. He is the seed in whom all blessings and revelations are made from God to man, and through whom man must come to the Father as he brings his petitions to Him.

Summary

In relation to the messianic hope: (1) Jesus confessed Himself to be the Messiah. (2) He acknowledged Himself to be the expected King. (3) He claimed to speak from God, hence, to be a

prophet, for His words were the words of God. (4) He claimed to
be the "Good Shepherd," the realization of the hope of the
messianic promises. (5) He confessed Himself to be the Son of
God in a special way. (6) He identified Himself as "the Son of
man," a new title, but one definitely related to the messianic
revelation of the prophets. (7) He claimed to be the Mediator
between God and man, and between man and God. These are
wonderful claims indeed! They are such that leave no question in
the mind of any man. Either He is Deity or He is a base impostor;
there can be no middle ground. He is not simply "a good man."
The question now is whether the evidence supports the claims in
sufficient strength that one can believe that He is what He claimed
to be.

His Relation to Human Needs 4

When Jesus came into the world, its needs were spiritual and moral, not physical and material. Although there were thousands who had not the bare necessities of life and were in abject poverty under oppression and in bondage, yet there were in the world all things necessary to provide for the physical life of all people. The universal need was for spiritual help and moral character to distribute and to use properly that which was here. Jesus came to provide this help.

Jesus made no direct attack on either the political or the social structure of His day; His attack was upon the sinful hearts of men and the sins which left men little more than beasts. His conviction was that if He could change the hearts of men and provide for their spiritual needs, man would change his circumstances. Unless the heart could be changed, sin erased, and man be given a master sentiment in life and an emotional impetus that would move him to act always in the right direction, then all social and political reforms would fail. Without this basic change, men would revert to their original status, even though their environment be improved. Jesus' concept of human needs and an objective in life is summed up in His own words when He said, "Work not for the food which perisheth, but for the food which abideth unto eternal life, which the Son of man shall give unto you: for him the Father, even God, hath sealed," that is, marked as reserved for this special distinction (6:27). This chapter is devoted to a consideration of some of the claims Jesus made for Himself in relation to human needs.

His Claim To Be the Revelation of God
(See Chapter 2)

When Jesus came into the world, its concept of true Godhood may be summed up in the one word *ignorance*. Although the Jews had the law and had been made the depository of divine revelation, they were ignorant of God's righteousness and had sought to establish their own (Rom. 10:1-4). The Gentiles, who had refused to have God in their knowledge and had abandoned themselves to idolatry and to the worship of creatures of their own imagination (Rom. 1:28, 18-23), were therefore ignorant of His unity. Paul ably pointed out this ignorance of the divine unity in his sermon on Mar's Hill (Acts 17:22-28). This ignorance of God, of His righteousness and of His unity, left both Jew and Gentile in need of a revelation of God—a revelation which they could see in action as He answered the needs of their hearts.

Philip voiced the cry of this universal need of the human heart when he said to Jesus, "Lord, show us the Father, and it sufficeth us" (14:8). Jesus had said to the group as He was preparing them for His going away, "If ye had known me, ye would have known my Father also: from henceforth ye know him, and have seen him" (14:7). In His reply to Philip, Jesus claimed that in Himself was a complete revelation of the Father when He said, "He that hath seen me hath seen the Father" (14:9). The words which He spoke and the works which He did were the words and works of the Father, words and works which the Father was doing through the Son (v. 10). "Believe me," said He, "that I am in the Father, and the Father in me: or else believe me for the very works' sake" (v. 11).

Jesus claimed that He was the revelation of God—the revelation of His Godhood or deity in all its fulness. There could be no attribute of God that was not summed up in Him. There was no expression of the fulness of Godhood that was lacking. In the words He spoke and the works He did God was revealing Himself.

As one listened and beheld, he could see the righteousness of God finding expression in Christ's love for the downtrodden, in His sacrifice for the lost, in His compassion for the suffering and despised, in His hatred and condemnation of sin, and in His disposition to restore men to their proper place with God. In these same words and works of Jesus, the unity of God is set before them in His oneness with God and in His disposition to do only that which pleases His Father. In His control over the forces of nature, whether on the sea or in the bodies of the suffering and afflicted, He was demonstrating a divine sovereignty and kinship with the Almighty One. In all realms He demonstrated the oneness of supreme power, whether physical or spiritual. In His reply to Philip, Jesus was claiming that He is the revelation of God to man, all-sufficient and complete. He was claiming to be the answer to this universal cry of all human hearts: "Lord, show us the Father and it sufficeth us."

His Claim To Be "the Way"

It is not enough that Jesus should reveal completely the Father in Himself; man must have a way by which he can come to the Father. Up to this point in human history man had possessed no means of direct access to God; now Jesus declares Himself to be that way. The destination is God; the way is Jesus Himself. Besides Him there is no other way or means of access.

As He had said to the Jews, so now Jesus said to the disciples as He was eating the supper with them immediately before His death: "Whither I go, ye cannot come" (13:33). He followed this with the assurance that in His Father's house there were many mansions, and that He would go and prepare a place for them, that where He would be there they may be also. He concluded with the statement, "And whither I go, ye know the way" (14:4). Thomas countered with the question, "Lord, we know not whither thou goest; how know we the way?" (v. 5). This question raised by Thomas appeared to have been a sigh of discouragement on the part of the disciple, as if to say, "Lord, you think we know; but actually, we do not." Jesus did not rebuke him, but said, "I (myself) am the way, and the truth, and the life: no one cometh unto the Father, but by me" (v. 6).

In glowing terms Isaiah had pictured the return of God's people to the Lord and the happy state of Zion. It would be in a time when the eyes of the blind should be opened and the ears of the deaf unstopped, when the lame should leap as a hart, and when the tongue of the dumb should sing. In the wilderness waters would break out and the glowing sand would become a pool. In the midst of this period, "A highway shall be there, and a way, and it shall be called The way of holiness; the unclean shall not pass over it; but it shall be for the redeemed: the wayfaring men, yea fools, shall not err therein" (Isa. 35:8). Though the passage is not mentioned, it seems evident that Jesus identified Himself with this Way as a supply to human need. He was the revelation of God, therefore holy; His call to men was to a way of holiness; only those who would believe on Him could be saved (8:24), and only through Him could men find access to the Father (14:6). Fools, that is, the depraved, the perverted, the abnormal, whose hearts speak folly (Isa. 32:5ff.), cannot come by Him. These must be completely transformed, or be excluded.

But more, He is "the truth, and the life." These seem to explain the first. He is "the way" because He is the embodiment of truth, in whom is no lie. God's truth, as over against Satan's lie (8:44), is summed up in Him. It is only as truth makes one free that man becomes free (8:32); and if "the Son shall make you free, ye shall be free indeed" (8:36). The Son therefore makes men free through truth, of which He is the embodiment and fulness. Only the free can abide in the house (8:35). Hence, it is as the Son, the embodiment and fulness of truth, that Jesus is the way to the Father and to freedom and permanence in His house.

Further, He is "the way" because He is the life, the divine life by which man is united with God. His claim had been, "For as the Father hath life in himself, even so gave he to the Son also to have life in himself" (5:26). On the ground of this relation with God, He said, "Even so the Son also giveth life to whom he will" (5:21). He is the way because only in Him who came from God, in whom is the divine life of God, is man united with the Father in His own eternal being. Jesus claimed that He is the answer to man's need for a way to the Father.

His Claim To Be Savior

When Jesus came into the world, man had no greater need than for a savior from sin. History, both secular and Biblical, bears witness to the moral depravity of man at that time and to his need for one to deliver him from such condition. The Jewish law had shown man what was right, but it had made no provision for his justification when that law was transgressed. Instead, it brought him under a curse (Deut. 27:26). Nor could the law offer him deliverance from sin's power, for the righteous should live by faith (Hab. 2:4). Gentile wisdom and philosophy had failed miserably, for all Gentiles were without God and without hope in the world. In hopeless despair they had abandoned themselves to the basest of idolatry that resulted in corruption, crime, and misery on every hand. Secular historians are as profuse in their description of the condition as is the apostle Paul in the first two chapters of Romans. Man *must* have a savior from such a state.

John introduced Jesus as "the Lamb of God, that taketh away the sin of the world" (1:29). The lamb was the victim offered at the morning and evening sacrifice (Exod. 29:38ff.); also it was the sacrifice that was eaten at the Passover each year. The most memorable deliverance in the history of the Jews was their deliverance from Egypt at the dawn of their national life when the first Paschal lamb had been slain. Now one was coming who would deliver from a greater bondage, the bondage of sin. But this lamb was not one provided by man; it was "the Lamb of God," that which God was providing. His mission would be to "take away the sin of the world." "Sin," singular, has regard for sin " in its unity" (Westcott). "Of the world" suggests the inclusiveness of His mission as it extended beyond the borders of the Jewish people to include all men.

Jesus' own claim was, "And as Moses lifted up the serpent in the wilderness, even so must the Son of man be lifted up; that whosoever believeth may in him have eternal life" (3:14f.). The words which followed (vv. 16-21) serve as a commentary to this claim. It was God's love which supplied the sacrifice; it would be faith that would appropriate it. Deliverance from perishing and the gift of eternal life would be the blessing (v. 16). The Son was sent not to judge but to save the world. However, His entrance into the world would be a judgment, for judgment would fall on the unbelievers whose love for darkness, rather than light, would hold them in unbelief (vv. 17-19). But to those who should seek to do the truth would come the light in which deliverance would be found.

Jesus saw sin as the bondage from which man must be delivered. According to Him, "Everyone that committeth sin is the bondservant of sin" (8:34), who, by his own will in gratifying his lusts, has made himself a child of Satan (8:44). And the bondservant could not deliver himself from his bondage nor make of himself a son; therefore he must be cast out. Only the Son could make him free (8:35f.). In the word *everyone* Jesus wiped out all distinction between Jew and Gentile; all who were under sin were bondservants of sin. They would die in that state of sin unless they would believe on Him (8:24). Clearly, He saw Himself as the Savior of man from sin, the Deliverer of man out of a bondage from which he could not deliver himself.

This deliverance would be offered through His death; He must be a lamb slain for sin. As the Passover, which would be the time when He would be offered, drew near, certain Greeks came to the feast and approached Philip with the request, "Sir, we would see Jesus" (12:21). Philip and Andrew came to Jesus presenting the request; He made reply, "The hour is come, that the Son of man should be glorified" (v. 23). It was too late for the Gentiles to be included in the teaching during His earthly ministry; it was too early for them to be brought into the completed work. Therefore Jesus replied, "And I, if I be lifted up from the earth, will draw *all men* unto myself"—this would include the Greeks as well as all others. "But this he said, signifying by what manner of death he should die" (vv. 32f.). The altar of sacrifice on which He would be offered would be a Roman cross (18:31ff.).

Another point needs to be considered here. When Jesus said, "The hour is come, that the Son of man should be glorified" (12:23), He then prayed, and God answered Him (vv. 27-30). Whereupon Jesus said, "Now is the judgment of this world: now shall the prince of this world be cast out" (v. 31). In judging Him and putting Him to death, the world was judging itself. And in His death, now at hand, and in His resurrection the world's prince was being cast out. The judgment of the world and the casting out of the prince of the world were intertwined with the salvation of man brought about by His being lifted up.

Shortly after this Jesus interrupted the conversation between Himself and His disciples by saying, "I will no more speak much with you, for the prince of the world cometh: and he hath nothing in me" (14:30). The Jewish rabble with Roman soldiers and

Jewish priests, all inspired by the very spirit of Satan, were coming for Him. But Satan had nothing in Him: He was guilty of no crime or violation of law; therefore, He could not be held by death. The casting out of Satan was so certain that Jesus assured them that the Spirit would convict the world of judgment, "because the prince of this world hath been judged" (16:11). In His provision for man's salvation through His meeting all needs for a Savior, Jesus condemned the world and cast Satan down from the place he had held until then. His claim was that He should bind Satan and that it would be done in His own triumph over death.

His Claim To Be Light

When Jesus came into the world, He found Himself in a world of darkness—darkness into which it had been plunged by sin. Isaiah's prediction was fully realized, for he had said, "Behold, darkness shall cover the earth, and gross darkness the peoples" (Isa. 60:2). There was a desperate need for light that would illuminate the lives of men, a light by which man could clearly determine what was right and what was sin. Now the long-awaited light was beginning to dawn. John had said of Him in the Prologue of his Gospel, "In him was life; and the life was the light of men. And the light shineth in the darkness; and the darkness apprehended it not" (1:4, 5). That divine life which was claimed for Jesus, and claimed by Him, would be the light which would kindle a brilliant glow in every man's soul (v. 9). It was a light that "the darkness apprehended not," that is, understood or comprehended it not (Alford, also Dods); or, overcame it not (Westcott). Both interpretations are true, but which idea John intended is not clear. The darkness of the world did not comprehend the light in Jesus, nor did the darkness "put it out," overcome it. History testifies that it has shone through the centuries, and experience testifies that it shines even now.

Jesus confirmed this claim made by John when He said, "I am the light of the world: he that followeth me shall not walk in the darkness, but shall have the light of life" (8:12). All that Jehovah had been to His people in the wilderness as He led them by the cloud by day and the pillar of fire by night, so Jesus would be to those who would follow Him. As the word had been to the psalmist (a lamp unto his feet and a light unto his path [Ps.

119:105], and when opened had given to him light and under-standing [v. 130]), so Jesus would be to all who should look to Him. And He would be even more, for in following Him one would have "the light of life"—eternal life.

When preparing to open the eyes of the man born blind, Jesus said, "When I am in the world, I am the light of the world" (9:5). In this statement the definite article is omitted; while in the world He is light to it. Later He said, "Yet a little while is the light among you. Walk while ye have the light, that darkness overtake you not: and he that walketh in the darkness knoweth not whither he goeth. While ye have the light, believe on the light, that ye may become sons of light" (12:35-36a). He would have men become sons of light, luminaries reflecting His own light in their lives, walking in the light, that they might have the life He came to provide.

Jesus concluded His claim as light when He said, "I am come a light into the world, that whosoever believeth on me may not abide in the darkness" (12:46). The world was in darkness; but if His claim be true, man would be at that time, and is today, without excuse for abiding in darkness. Jesus claimed to be the embodiment of all spiritual and moral light, light brought into the world from without, brought from above, that men might have the light of life.

His Claim To Be the Provider of Spiritual Sustenance

Prior to the coming of Jesus, the human family had sought to feed the spirit on the husks of human philosophy on the one hand and on traditions and legalistic observances of law on the other. Both had failed; man was in a state of spiritual malnutrition. In the midst of such spiritual and moral sickness, Jesus claimed that He had come that "they may have life, and may have it abun-dantly" (10:10). This life of which He spoke was spiritual or eternal life. Once it exists, life, whether physical, vegetable, or spiritual, must be sustained by nourishment which befits the particular life. Jesus claimed three things for Himself in relation to spiritual nurture: He is the water of life, also the bread of life, and He is the true vine through which is provided the nourishment for fruit bearing.

The Water of Life. To the woman at Sychar in Samaria, from whom Jesus had requested a drink from Jacob's well, He said, "If thou knewest the gift of God, and who it is that saith to thee, Give me to drink; thou wouldest have asked of him, and he would have given thee living water" (4:10). In the discussion which followed, Jesus said of the water from the well, "Every one that drinketh of this water shall thirst again: but whosoever drinketh of the water that I shall give him shall never thirst; but the water that I shall give him shall become in him a well of water springing up unto eternal life" (4:13f.). The water that Jesus claimed to provide is spiritual, heavenly, and permanent, not material, earthly, and transient. It lives on as a spring within one, constantly refreshing and forever at hand.

Upon another occasion, while attending the feast of tabernacles, Jesus cried, saying, "If any man thirst, let him come unto me and drink." As God had provided water for the thirsty travelers through the wilderness in ancient days, so now Christ proposes to provide in a higher sense the spiritual water for man's soul. To the woman in Samaria (ch. 4) Jesus had promised personal satisfaction in that which He would provide; now He promises that those who drink would not only be satisfied themselves, but they would also be able to provide for the wants of others, for "from within him (the believer) shall flow rivers of living water" (7:37-39).

The Bread of Life. After Jesus had spent a day teaching, He fed the multitude of five thousand men with five barley loaves and two fishes. This incident led to His discourse on "the bread of life." The multitude sought Him out the next day that they might again be filled with loaves and fishes, but Jesus was interested in food of an entirely different nature. His concern was for food which sustains spiritual life. On the morrow in the synagogue at Capernaum, they asked for other signs, calling attention to the feeding of the fathers in the wilderness by Moses. Jesus assured them that it was not Moses who fed the fathers, but His Father, and that it was the Father who would now feed them "true bread out of heaven. For the bread of God is that which cometh down out of heaven, and giveth life unto the world" (6:32f.). Immediately they requested that He give them this bread. He responded by making the claim, "I am the bread of life: he that cometh to me shall not hunger, and he that believeth on me shall never thirst" (6:35). His claim to being the water that quenches spiritual thirst is now paralleled by the claim that He is the bread from God which gives life and appeases spiritual hunger.

This claim led to murmuring among the Jews, giving Jesus opportunity to say that this bread would enable one to eat and not die, and to affirm, "I am the living bread which came down out of heaven: if any man eat of this bread, he shall live for ever: yea and the bread which I will give is my flesh, for the life of the world" (v. 51). The remainder of the chapter is a discussion of the bread and of life, and of the result that developed in the attitude of the people. Our concern just here is in the claim made by Jesus in relation to the spiritual needs of man; He claimed that He was the bread of life and that those who should eat of that bread would not hunger.

The Vine and the Branches. Another claim made by Jesus as the provider for human needs is that He is the vine through whom each branch derives the living sap essential to bearing fruit. "I am the true vine" (15:1) is His claim made to the disciples the night of His betrayal. It is only by abiding in Him, and His word abiding in them, that they would be able to bear fruit; and it is by bearing fruit that the Father should be glorified by them (vv. 4-8).

As the true vine, He would sustain them perfectly. In Him the union with deity would be perfectly realized. The disciples would experience the fulfilling of their prayers to God, the divine joy of Jesus would be theirs, and God would be glorified (vv. 8-10). The ultimate completeness in discipleship would be realized in this union with Him.

His Claim To Be Shepherd and King

Jesus' claim to be king and shepherd in relation to the messianic hope has been pointed out. But a word needs to be added regarding this claim in its relation to human needs. Jeremiah had long before cried, "O Jehovah, I know that the way of man is not in himself; it is not in man that walketh to direct his steps" (Jer. 10:23). The history of Israel, and of all mankind, had demonstrated this truth. Man needed—and needs—a shepherd to guide him through pleasant pastures and by placid streams and to provide for him a shelter in time of storm and a fold wherein is found protection.

Also, man needed a king to give him courage and leadership and to lead him to victory and triumph in the forays of life. The common people among the Jews had long been under the spiritual domination of the Pharisees and religious leaders in Jerusalem. The contempt in which the people were held by those in Jerusalem was clearly stated when they said to the officers sent to arrest Jesus, "Hath any of the rulers believed on him, or of the Pharisees? But this multitude that knoweth not the law are accursed" (7:48-49). The people needed a leader who would give them courage to stand up in the force of opposition and error and who would declare their conviction for what was right. They needed a king on whom they could rely, who would provide this essential courage, and who would then lead them to victory in the conflict which was sure to follow. Jesus claimed to be the answer to these very desperate needs of the human family. The Gentiles would be included, for He would draw "all men" unto Himself (12:32).

"I am the good shepherd: the good shepherd layeth down his life for the sheep" (10:11). He was no hireling; He cared for His sheep. He knew them, they knew Him, and He was willing to lay down His life for them (vv. 11-15). His sheep would follow Him, and He would give them eternal life. They would never perish but would enjoy constant protection; no man or wild beast would be able to snatch them out of His hand (vv. 27f.). As a shepherd He represented the Father who is greater than all, and no man was able to snatch the sheep out of His Father's hand (v. 29).

In response to Pilate's question, "Art thou a king then?" Jesus had answered, "Thou sayest that I am a king" (18:37a), which is to say, "Thou art right, for a king I am" (Dods). But He was king of a world different from that of Pilate. He continued, "To this end have I been born, and to this end am I come into the world, that I should bear witness unto the truth. Every one that is of the truth heareth my voice" (v. 37b). He was king of truth; He came to lead men in a moral and spiritual warfare in which truth would be the power of conquest and victory. There were plenty of Caesars to lead them in their military campaigns. Jesus was king of a different realm; His weapon was not of this world—His weapon was truth.

His Claim To Be the Resurrection

The great pyramids of Egypt are monuments to man's effort to provide for the future life. Buried with the pharaohs in these magnificent tombs were articles and servants to be used in the next world. From these gigantic tombs of one of the greatest of ancient civilizations to the burying grounds of the prehistoric American Indians, one finds artifacts buried with the dead to be used by them in the next life. All of these are mute witnesses to man's desire to live beyond this life; but until the coming of Jesus Christ, there was no clear positive voice that carried assurance of such life. Man needed a sure note on which he could hang his hope for something beyond. He needed assurance of a resurrection. In response to this age-old longing of the human heart, Jesus promised that to those who should believe on Him He would give eternal life and raise them up at the last day (6:39ff., 44, 54).

However, this power to raise the dead was to be demonstrated in Himself. When challenged by the Jews for a sign when He cleansed the temple, Jesus replied, "Destroy this temple, and in three days I will raise it up... But he spake of the temple of his body" (2:19-21). This, He assured them, would be the supreme sign of His relation to God and His true temple. He further claimed, "I lay down my life, that I may take it again. No one taketh it away from me, but I lay it down of myself. I have power to lay it down, and I have power to take it again" (10:17f.). In His ability to do this He would demonstrate this final and supreme claim which relates Him to the longing and need of humanity, "I am the resurrection, and the life: he that believeth on me, though he die, yet shall he live; and whosoever liveth and believeth on me shall never die" (11:25f.). In this statement two claims are made: "(1) that resurrection and life are not future only, but present; and (2) that they become ours by union with Christ" (Dods). He is the resurrection and life in person. Any hope of resurrection and life beyond this life is in Him, and apart from Him there is nought but death and despair. This is His claim.

Summary

In His claims with respect to human needs, Jesus claimed (1) to be the revelation of God, that God was in Him speaking His words and doing His works; that He is (2) the way of life, (3) the Savior of men, (4) the light of the world, (5) the sustaining power of life, (6) the shepherd and king, and (7) the resurrection and the life. These claims, if sustained, prove Him to be the divine Son of God.

If they are not sustained, He is convicted of being the greatest fraud ever to impose himself on the human family. Claims of Jesus in His relation to God, to the messianic hope, and to human needs, as set forth in the Gospel of John, have been briefly sketched. The evidence to sustain the claims, as presented by John, will be the theme of the remainder of this book.

PART TWO

Testimony Offered

to Sustain the Claims of Jesus

Human 5 Testimony

John's purpose in writing his Gospel was that men might believe that Jesus is the Christ and, through that belief in Him, have eternal life. Since all belief rests on evidence, John has presented the testimony which he believed would beget and sustain such faith. His Gospel is not a biography of the life of Jesus. Instead, John selects incidents and teaching from about twenty of the approximate one thousand days of Jesus' ministry and offers this evidence to prove his proposition.

The testimony to the deity of Jesus as presented in the Gospel of John falls under two heads: Human and Divine. The human testimony also falls into two divisions: that of John the Baptist, and that of those who came in contact with Jesus. Some may object to the identification of the Baptist's testimony as human testimony on the ground that "he was a man sent from God." Both John the immerser and John the apostle recognized that the commission of the baptizer was a divine commission. However, Jesus said, "Ye have sent unto John, and he hath borne witness unto the truth. But the witness which I receive is not from man ... The witness which I have is greater than that of John ...

the Father that sent me, he hath borne witness of me" (5:33-37). Jesus said that John was "a man," and that the witness Jesus had was greater than that of John the Baptist, whose testimony will be included in the section of human testimony. John the Baptist's testimony will, however, be presented as distinct from that of all other human witness, because he was sent by Jehovah with a special commission.

The Testimony of John the Baptist

The writer of the Fourth Gospel passes over a discussion of the parentage, birth, and desert life of John. He makes no mention of John's relation to Jesus or of his conversation with Jesus when He came to John to be baptized. Likewise, he passes over John's preaching of the nearness of the kingdom, the call to repentance, and the meaning he attached to it. Also, he passes over the untimely death of the forerunner of Jesus.

The evangelist presents the scene of John's ministry as being "Bethany (or Bethabarah) beyond the Jordan" (1:28), and "Aenon near to Salim" (3:23); the location of both places is now unknown. It may be inferred from the disciples' use of "beyond the Jordan" (3:26) that John spent some time in Peraea (i.e., "land beyond the Jordan"). Other than these references, he says nothing of places covered by John.

John (the apostle) testified to the divine mission of the baptizer (1:6), which the forerunner also claimed for himself (1:33). He acknowledged the superiority of Jesus to himself as one, "the latchet of whose shoe I am not worthy to unloose" (1:27). He recognized himself as "the friend of the bridegroom," in whose voice he rejoiced, and he acknowledged the temporary character of his work in comparison to that of Jesus when he said, "He must increase, but I must decrease" (3:30).

The work of John the Baptist was twofold: (1) to proclaim the approaching nearness of the kingdom of heaven, and to prepare a people for it, and (2) to bear formal testimony to Jesus as the Son of God. The evangelist passes silently over the first of these, using only that part of John's testimony and work that sustains his proposition: Jesus is the Christ, the Son of God. "There came a man, sent from God, whose name was John. The same came for witness, that he might bear witness of the light, that all might believe through him" (1:6, 7)—believe through John's testimony that Jesus was the Messiah.

The character and purpose of the Fourth Gospel is indicated by the number of times (33) John uses the verb *martureo*, "bear witness, testify concerning someone or something."[1] The word is translated "bear witness, bear record, testify." The noun *marturia*, "a bearing witness,"[2] is used fourteen times in the Gospel and sixteen times in John's other writings; it is used only seven times by all other writers of the New Testament. The word more fully defined means "(to give) competent testimony concerning that which one has himself seen, heard, or experienced."[3] It is said, "In ancient days, as at present, this was a legal term designating the testimony given for or against one on trial before a court of law."[4] The mission of John, the forerunner of Jesus, was to bear witness, give competent testimony as for one on trial, to that which he had seen and heard from God concerning the Messiah, Jesus.

The testimony of John (the Baptist) begins with testimony concerning himself, which clarified his mission or office and his relation to his work. His testimony was both negative and positive. When questioned by a deputation of priests and Levites sent out from Jerusalem to ask him, "Who art thou?" his answer was negative in its nature. To their question concerning his being the Christ, he said, "I am not the Christ" (1:20). To the next question, "Art thou Elijah?" the reply was again negative, "I am not" (1:21a). And in answering the third question, "Art thou the prophet?" he was even more brief; the answer was "No" (1:21b). But these men sent out to him from Jerusalem must have an answer to take back with them. If he was not the Christ, neither Elijah, nor the prophet, they must determine who he was. This time the answer was positive: "I am the voice of one crying in the wilderness, Make straight the way of the Lord, as said Isaiah the prophet" (1:23). John's negative testimony of himself was that he was not the Christ, Elijah, or the prophet. The positive testimony

---

1. Arndt and Gingrich, p. 498.
2. W. E. Vine, *An Expository Dictionary of New Testament Words*, Vol. IV, p. 225.
3. W. Hendriksen, *New Testament Commentary, An Exposition of the Gospel According to John*, Vol. I, p. 76.
4. Baker's *Dictionary of Theology*, p. 555.

was that he was simply "voice," the definite article being omitted in the original. John's testimony of himself was who he was not, and who he was.

This reply identified John with the hope of one of the great "comfort" chapters of Isaiah, which told of the greatness of Israel's incomparable God, who would pardon the iniquities of His people (Isa. 40:1-2). Following the promise that He would pardon His people, the Lord had said, "And the glory of Jehovah shall be revealed, and all flesh shall see it together" (Isa. 40:5). But the voice of one preparing the way for the revelation of this "glory" would precede the coming of the glory (Isa. 40:3-4). John claimed to be that voice, thereby identifying himself with prophecy as the forerunner and herald of the messianic "glory." If the "voice" was now being heard, the "glory" would not be long in appearing. In the Prologue of the Gospel, the writer affirms that this glory was summed up in its fulness in the Incarnate Word (1:14, 16).

John's testimony to the Christ as presented in the early part of the book was to three groups: to the deputation sent out from Jerusalem; to a group before him, apparently where he was preaching and baptizing; and to two of his disciples.

(1) His testimony to the Jews from Jerusalem was that he was the voice which fulfilled the prophecy of Isaiah as the one who should introduce Jehovah's "glory." Indirectly, therefore, his testimony was that Jesus was "the glory" that should appear among all flesh. He further testified, "in the midst of you standeth one whom ye know not, even he that cometh after me, the latchet of whose shoe I am not worthy to unloose" (1:26f.). When associated with his claim to be the voice foretold by Isaiah, this statement testified that the Messiah, far greater than himself, as "the glory of Jehovah," was about to appear.

(2) On the morrow, to a crowd possibly more keenly alert than usual to the excitement of John's preaching, John testified, "Behold, the Lamb of God, that taketh away the sin of the world!" (1:29). This identified Jesus as the sacrificial hope of the Old Covenant, as the sacrifice itself; this was a sacrifice to be shared not by Jews only, but also by "the whole world." As "all flesh" should see the glory (Isa. 40:5), so all "the world" should share in the sacrifice. In bearing this witness, John was testifying that as the Lamb of God Jesus was fulfilling another prophecy of Isaiah,

"As a lamb that is led to the slaughter, and as a sheep that before its shearers is dumb, so he opened not his mouth . . . who among them considered that he was cut off out of the land of the living for the transgression of my people to whom the stroke was due" (Isa. 53:7f.).

John had known Him as "the glory" and "the Lamb"; he knew only that such a one was to be manifested and that he would recognize Him by testimony from heaven. The testimony to John from God was the descent of the Holy Spirit as a dove upon Him at His baptism. John then testified that the Holy Spirit had descended upon Him when he had baptized Him, therefore, "I have seen, and have borne witness that this is the Son of God" (1:34).

Again, "on the morrow," as John was standing with two of his disciples he saw Jesus coming, and, as he had said to the crowd on the day before, he now repeated, "Behold, the Lamb of God!" (1:36). These two disciples left him to follow Jesus.

(3) John's final testimony was borne sometime later when one of his disciples came to him with the complaint that the one to whom he had borne witness was now baptizing, "and all men come to him" (3:26). John's reply was that he had borne witness that he himself was not the Christ but that he was sent before Him; his joy would be made full because the one's voice to whom he had borne witness was now being heard. And then he spoke his parting testimony, "He must increase, but I must decrease" (3:30). Truly, this is the testimony of a magnanimous spirit. He had fulfilled his mission of bearing witness to the Light, and now he was ready to retire from the limelight of popularity in favor of that one.

John the Baptist's testimony to the deity of Jesus may be summed up under five heads: (1) He is the "glory" that was to come, the glory of God in human flesh; (2) He is "the Lamb of God that taketh away the sin of the world"; (3) He is "the Son of God," for to this God had borne witness (1:33-34); (4) He "was before me"; and (5) "He must increase, but I must decrease." In recognition of a job well done, Jesus paid him a tribute of greatness when He said, "Ye have sent unto John, and he hath borne witness unto the truth: . . . He was the lamp that burneth and shineth; and ye were willing to rejoice for a season in his light" (5:33, 35). He was a true light, bearing witness to the truth.

The Testimony of Those Who
Came in Contact with Jesus

The testimony of all other human witnesses presented by John in his Gospel differs from that of John the Baptist. As pointed out above, John's witness was one sent from God, fulfilling prophecy, and confirmed from heaven in the form of the Holy Spirit's descent upon the Lord; whereas, the testimony of all other witnesses is the testimony of an impression made on the witnesses by their contact with Jesus. The testimony of and within itself does not prove any claim made by Jesus to be true, whether the claims were regarding His relation to God and to the messianic hope, or His fulfillment of all human needs of a spiritual nature. Their witness testifies only to the weight and effect of Jesus' teaching, works, and claims upon those who saw and heard Him. The evidence is circumstantial and incidental, but it is worthy of a candid and fair consideration. The value of human testimony has been well summarized by another who, in writing of the weight of apostolic testimony, said,

> The force of human testimony depends on three things: first, the honesty of the witnesses; second, their competency; and third, their number. We ascertain whether they are honest, by considering their general character and their motives in the particular case. . . . Competency is determined by considering the opportunities of the witness to obtain knowledge of that to which he testifies, and his mental capacity to observe and remember the facts. The requisite number varies with the degree of probability attached to the facts.[5]

The witness of fifteen groups or individuals will be presented as John records their testimony. In the case of most of these, little comment will be made. The witnesses will be left to speak for themselves.

1. The early disciples

When the two disciples heard John the Baptist testify, "Behold! the Lamb of God" (1:36), they followed Jesus. Jesus invited them to come with Him to the place where He was abiding, and they spent the remainder of the day in His company. These two were so impressed that one of them, Andrew, found his brother

---

5. J. W. McGarvey, *Evidences of Christianity*, Book II, p. 146.

Simon, to whom he said, "We have found the Messiah" (1:41). The testimony of John and what Andrew himself saw in Jesus so favorably fulfilled his expectation of what the Messiah should be that he was convinced.

On the next day Jesus found Philip, who followed Him upon the simple invitation, "Follow me." Philip immediately sought Nathanael, to whom he enthusiastically bare witness, "We have found him, of whom Moses in the law, and the prophets, wrote" (1:45).

Nathanael was not impressed. But when he came to meet Jesus and heard Him tell of his former activities, Nathanael was so stirred that he answered, "Rabbi, thou art the Son of God; thou art King of Israel" (1:49). The impression of these three early disciples was that Jesus was the Messiah, of whom Moses and the prophets had written, the Son of God, the King of Israel. Their testimony does not prove that He was any one of these, but it does bear witness to the impression that Jesus made upon them. There is no evidence that any one of the group ever retracted the impressions or denied them. The impressions grew into assured conviction and remained through life.

2. Mary, the mother of Jesus

The testimony of Mary is incidental, not direct, both in statement and in her silence. At the marriage feast in Cana of Galilee, attended by Mary, Jesus, and His disciples, the wine failed. One can imagine the embarrassment of guests with such considerate feelings as Mary and Jesus possessed. Moved by her first impulse, Mary said to Jesus, "They have no wine." Jesus' reply was to impress her with the realization that what He should do from thence would be by the guiding hand of a greater and higher than she. Immediately she turned to the servants and said, "Whatsoever he saith unto you, do it" (2:1-5). Her words and actions imply the knowledge and assurance that Jesus was more than merely another guest at the feast; He was one who could cope with the situation. The testimony is circumstantial or incidental, but it is challenging.

Once more she bare witness, but this time by her silence. As Mary stood at the foot of the cross upon which her beloved son had been nailed, she heard Him make provision for her care in the home of the disciple whom He loved. What a heart-rending experience it must have been for this one who carried so many secrets in her heart to behold Him in such pain, yet to hear Him make provision for her welfare while oblivious to His own. As she had seen tension, hatred, and bitterness mounting among the people, and the determination of His enemies to put Him to death, one word from her would have saved Him from the hour. One word, "This is not the Son of God! _____ is his father," would have cleared Him. Imagine the piercing sense of guilt, a guilt akin to that of murder, that would have been hers if He were not what He had claimed to be! Only she knew positively whether He was the Son of God or a bastard, and there she stood, silently allowing Him to be crucified under the charge, "he made himself the Son of God" (19:7). Either He was what He had claimed to be, or Mary takes her place among the arch-criminals of history, confederate to a conspiracy of hypocrisy, deceit, blasphemy, imposture, and fanaticism. But reason asks what motive could she have had for all this? Echo answers, what? There she stood, silent. But what volumes that silence speaks! It is mute testimony to the claim that Jesus had made, "I am from above: . . . I am not of this world" (8:23). Surely the tenderness, character, and love of Mary for Jesus would equal that of the harlot who, when Solomon would divide the living babe between the mother and another, cried, "Oh, my lord, give her the living child, and in no wise slay it" (I Kings 3:26). The nobility of true motherhood here hangs in the balance as Mary keeps silent. Here also hangs the difference between the blackness of falsehood and the character of truth.

3. Nicodemus

In the early ministry of Jesus, when He made His first trip to Jerusalem, Nicodemus was so impressed by His teaching that he came to Him by night to hear and learn more from this one who so courageously had done what any honorable Jew should have done. Jesus had begun His work there by casting out the animals and moneychangers and by overturning the tables of these men as they made the temple grounds of Jehovah's house a house of merchandise. Nicodemus was a ruler of the Jews, a Pharisee, a man of no mean position and reputation in the city. He introduced himself to Jesus with the testimony, "Rabbi, we know that thou art a teacher come from God; for no one can do these signs that thou doest, except God be with him" (3:2).

The faith of these Jerusalem believers may have been superficial, light, fickle, but there is no indication that Nicodemus ever wavered from the belief here expressed. Before his own company of Pharisees, he proved himself to be a man of fair dealings with another when he defended Jesus' right to be heard (7:50-51). We may never know whether he ever had the courage to confess that faith and make it a living, dynamic force in his life; but the fact that he came with Joseph to ask for the body of Jesus that it might be given a decent burial (19:39) testifies to the fact that he never wavered from the testimony borne upon his first meeting with the Master Teacher: "Rabbi, ... thou art a teacher come from God."

4. The Samaritans

In His conversation with the woman at the well near Sychar, Jesus so impressed her by His conversation and insight into her own private life that she said, "Sir, I perceive that thou art a prophet" (4:19). So excited was she by the conversation that followed that she left her waterpot and hurried to the city, where she said to the people, "Come, see a man, who told me all things that ever I did: can this be the Christ?" (4:29). She made no affirmation other than that He had told her things of her life which He could not have known by former acquaintance. She then raised the question, "Can this be the Christ" for whom the Samaritans were looking? The woman showed her insight into human nature by this approach; for a question properly posed could arouse more interest than anything else she could have said.

The testimony of the woman, "He told me all things that ever I did" (4:39), led to an invitation from the people that Jesus spend some time with them. At the close of two days in their midst, the Samaritans were so impressed that they said to the woman, "Now we believe, not because of thy speaking: for we have heard for ourselves, and know that this is indeed the Saviour of the world" (v. 42). Their contact with Jesus had led them to a deeper faith that Jesus was the Savior of the world based on first-hand knowledge which they now had. Based on their contact with Jesus, the woman and her Samaritan associates testified that "He told me all things that ever I did," and, "This is indeed the Saviour of the world."

5. Peter

At the close of the day which he had spent teaching the multitude, Jesus fed the five thousand men, besides women and children, with five small loaves and two fishes. The people were so impressed that they were ready to take Jesus by force and make Him king (6:15). On the morrow Jesus followed this miracle with the sermon on the bread of life. He was sifting the multitude, testing them to see whether they would accept Him as a spiritual Messiah and not as a political king. At the close of the address, many said, "This is a hard saying; who can hear it?" (6:60). Jesus continued His explanation by assuring them that it was not the flesh but the spirit that profits and gives life, and that the words which He spoke were spirit and life (v. 63). This only confused them the more, whereupon "many of his disciples went back, and walked no more with him" (v. 66).

Jesus had proved His point; they were not ready for a spiritual Messiah, the king of a kingdom not of this world. But instead of running after the departing disciples in a further effort to explain His teaching, Jesus turned to the twelve and asked, "Would ye also go away?" (v. 67). As Peter spoke for the eleven as well as for himself, his reply revealed the impression Jesus had made on them, "Lord, to whom shall we go? thou hast the words of eternal life. And we have believed and know that thou art the Holy One of God" (vv. 68f). Later, in a moment of weakness, Peter denied acquaintance with the Lord; but from the conviction here stated he never wavered. He gave his life to the proclamation of these words which he believed to be "unto eternal life."

6. The multitude

The opinion of the multitude was divided; consequently, they give a divided testimony. With some the testimony borne would be prejudiced by the influence of the Jewish rulers on their thinking. Others, who had not been so prejudiced, could bear a more unbiased witness. After they had beheld the feeding of the five thousand with the few loaves and fishes, the people were ready to take Him by force and crown Him king. The next day after the feeding of the five thousand and the attempt to take Him by force and make Him king, the testimony of some was, "Is not this Jesus, the son of Joseph, whose father and mother we know?" (6:42). They could accept His miracle, but they could not accept His deity. Sometime following the feeding of the five thousand, Jesus went up to Jerusalem to the feast of tabernacles. This feast would be attended by Jews not only from Galilee but also from all over the world. Many of these would know of Jesus by hearsay. Others would be from among those who had seen and heard Him personally. Jews from among these groups sought Him as they raised the question, "Where is he?" (7:11). Opinion was divided because many had not had sufficient opportunity to hear and see Him. Some said, "He is a good man," while others said, "Not so, but he leadeth the multitude astray" (v. 12).

As the multitude saw and heard Jesus during the days of the feast, opinions based upon more solid evidence became more definite. Some raised the question, "Can it be that the rulers indeed know that this is the Christ?" (7:26). As Jesus continued His teaching, the rulers sought to lay hands on Him, "But of the multitude many believed on him; and they said, When the Christ shall come, will he do more signs than those which this man hath done?" (7:31). Impressions were becoming more concrete.

Feelings among the Jews mounted as Jesus continued to teach. The rulers were becoming determined to get rid of Him. The opinions of the multitudes were beginning to take definite form. Some said, "This is of a truth the prophet." Others said, "This is the Christ." But some said, "What, doth the Christ come out of Galilee? Hath not the scripture said that the Christ cometh of the seed of David, and from Bethlehem, the village where David was? So there arose a division in the multitude because of him" (7:40-43). The testimony of these, even though they were divided over whether He was the prophet or the Christ, or over their uncertain knowledge of the place of His nativity, recognized that an extraordinary person was in their midst. One thing was certain: He was no mere teacher of the school of the rabbis.

Some months later when the multitude had come to Jerusalem for the Passover, they revealed their impression of Jesus by their demonstration as He entered the city. Hearing that Jesus was coming from Bethany, they "took the branches of the palm trees, and went forth to meet him, and cried out, Hosanna: Blessed is he that cometh in the name of the Lord, even the King of Israel" (12:13). This was the testimony of the multitude at this particular time. They saw in Jesus the fulfillment of their long cherished dream of a Messiah. His popularity was at its peak. However, within the week the voice of the Jerusalem Jews had prevailed over that of the out-of-town multitude, and their voice was heard before Pilate as they cried, "Away with him, away with him, crucify him!" To this the chief priests added their word of rejection, "We have no king but Caesar" (19:15).

The testimony of the multitude may be summed up as that of confusion and division at first; later some confessed and acclaimed that He was their King and some completely rejected Him.

7. The Jews

Except for the Book of Acts, which refers often to "Jew" or "Jews," John, in his Gospel, uses the word more than all other writers of the New Testament combined. Almost always, when speaking of "Jews," John refers to those from the environs of Jerusalem. The apostle came to look upon the Jews and to refer to them as a body of men hostile to Christ during His ministry and to His disciples later. He saw nothing in common between the two groups (Thayer, p. 306).

Their testimony is interesting. First, they marveled at His teaching, but they were puzzled over the source of His learning: "The Jews therefore marvelled, saying, How knoweth this man letters, having never learned?" (7:15). This was an admission that they recognized His superior knowledge of Jewish letters.

Later, divisions over His teaching arose among this group similar to those that had arisen among the multitude. "Many of them said, He hath a demon, and is mad; why hear ye him? Others said, These are not the sayings of one possessed with a demon. Can a demon open the eyes of the blind?" (10:20-21). By this testimony they convict themselves as being prejudiced and unfair in their judgment, for they clearly admit that the eyes of a blind man had been opened. This they do not deny. Also, they confess or admit that they look upon demons as being in league with that which is evil and antagonistic to the good. This was their point in saying that Jesus had a demon and was mad; the two were incompatible.

They charged Jesus with acting by the power of a demon, and yet doing a supernatural deed of goodness in opposition to the work of demons, by which they said He did the deed. Thus they were utterly inconsistent in their reasoning. The value of their testimony is in their admission of the sign and in revealing their own prejudice, which kept them from acknowledging their recognition of His deity.

8. The Pharisees

The testimony of the Pharisees as witness to Jesus' works and influence, like that of the multitude and the Jews, is of interest because they, too, were divided. They testify to three things:

First, they testify to the signs that Jesus had done. When confronted with the problems of the blind man whose sight had been restored, they admitted the sign but were divided over the source of the sign (9:16). After the raising of Lazarus from the dead, they gathered a council and said, "What do we? for this man doeth many signs" (11:47). Their witness is not that Jesus had given only one sign, but many. It is strange that they never denied the miracles. They denied only the source of the signs; and at this point they were not competent to testify, for they were not in position to know the source. They could see the miracles, and to these they bore testimony; they should not have put themselves in the unenviable position of assuming their diabolic origin.

Second, they testified to Jesus' influence upon the people and to their fear of the results of His work. In connection with the above statement, they said, "If we let him thus alone, all men will believe on him: and the Romans will come and take away both our place and our nation" (v. 48).

Third, they confessed their own failure in being able to cope with Him and with the situation that had arisen. Each sought to accuse the other: they said among themselves, "Behold how ye prevail nothing; lo, the world is gone after him" (12:19). They admitted their frustration and also revealed their dishonesty.

The witness of the Pharisees was: He has done many signs; His influence is mounting; nothing we have done has been able to stem the tide of His popularity. When all efforts had failed, there remained one alternative: they could put Him to death. From that time they began to carry out their diabolical plan. "Ye know

nothing at all," said Caiaphas to them, "nor do ye take account
that it is expedient for you that one man should die for the
people, and that the whole nation perish not" (11:49-50). From
that time they took counsel how they might put Him to death.

9. The officers

While Jesus was in Jerusalem for the feast of tabernacles, He
made such an impression on the multitude that the Pharisees
became alarmed. They sent officers, "servants or officers of the
Sanhedrin" (Thayer), to arrest Jesus. They returned without Him.
When asked why they had not brought Him, the officers could
only offer the explanation, "Never man so spake" (7:46). This was
tacit witness that Jesus had deeply impressed them; He had so
completely amazed them that they were unable to allow themselves to take Him. They had never heard teaching such as this
man was doing! Their testimony was, "Never man so spake." This
led to the explosive retort of the Pharisees, "Are ye also led
astray?"

10. The man born blind

It seems that Jesus often chose deliberately, even delightedly, to
perform His miracles on the sabbath. Doing such works on the
sabbath in no way violated the law of the sabbath. But what He
did aroused indignation among the Pharisees because it violated
their traditions concerning the sabbath.

One of His sabbath day miracles was healing a man born blind.
While in the city for the feast of tabernacles, Jesus performed this
extraordinary sign, which aroused the interest of the man's neighbors and the indignation of the Pharisees. Jesus anointed the eyes
of the man with clay and then told him to go wash in the pool of
Siloam. Some among the group of interested spectators brought
the man to the Pharisees, who asked him how he had received his
sight. He related the account to them, causing division among
them over the character of Him by whom the sign had been
wrought. They asked the man for his opinion of Him who had
opened his eyes; to this request he replied, "He is a prophet"
(9:17).

The Pharisees were not satisfied with the man's testimony; they
called for his parents, who, for fear of the Jews, refused to testify
further than that he was their son and that he had been born

blind. They then called for the man whose eyes were now opened and charged him to "Give glory to God: we know that this man is a sinner" (v. 24). This charge was made without testimony other than that Jesus had healed the man on the sabbath. To this the man answered, "Whether he is a sinner, I know not: one thing I know, that, whereas I was blind, now I see" (v. 25). The Pharisees responded by asking him a second time how he had been healed; to this request he chided them by asking if they, too, would like to become His disciples. The Pharisees replied by claiming to be disciples of Moses and to know from whence Moses had come but not to know from whence Jesus had come. The man made answer that the marvel was that they did not know from whence Jesus had come, and yet He had opened his eyes. This evidence pointed to the fact that Jesus was not a sinner but a worshiper of God and that if He was not from God, He could do nothing. After this testimony the Pharisees cast him out.

Later Jesus found him whom they had cast out and asked him, "Dost thou believe on the Son of God?" (v. 35). The man asked who is He that he might believe, to which Jesus replied, "Thou hast both seen him, and he it is that speaketh with thee." To this the man answered, "Lord, I believe. And he worshipped him" (v. 38).

The testimony of this man may be summed up as follows: (1) "I was born blind"; (2) I see; (3) the evidence points to the fact that Jesus is a prophet; (4) that He is a worshipper of God; (5) that He is one who does God's will; (6) that He came from God; and (7) that, therefore, He is the Son of God.

11. Martha and Mary

Jesus had spent much time in the home of Martha and Mary and their brother Lazarus. He considered them as special friends. Their opportunity to observe Him and His words and conduct had been full and complete. Having lived in the vicinity of Jerusalem, they had been given ample opportunity to be influenced by the Jews in their thinking. The testimony of these two women is straightforward and to the point.

Lazarus, their brother, had been sick; wherefore, they had sent for Jesus. Before He came, Lazarus had died. As Jesus drew near the home of the sisters, someone told Martha that Jesus was coming; immediately she arose and went to meet Him. Her first statement was one of confidence and of testimony to her faith,

though yet imperfect, in His power. Had He been present He could
have prevented the death: "Lord, if thou hadst been here, my
brother had not died" (11:21). When Mary came to meet Him, her
words were the same (v. 32). Martha's second word of confidence
was, "And even now I know that, whatsoever thou shalt ask of
God, God will give thee" (v. 22). Probably she had seen this
demonstrated at times previous when she had heard Jesus ask and
had seen the divine response. Jesus replied, "Thy brother shall rise
again" (v. 23). Martha's third testimony to her faith was, "I know
that he shall rise again in the resurrection at the last day" (v. 24).
This expressed an imperfect faith, for if Jesus could have prevented the death of Lazarus, could He not raise Him even now?
Jesus' reply seems to have been a reproof of her wavering belief.
He assured her that He was the resurrection and the life; Martha
then expressed her ultimate confidence and faith in Him when she
said, "Yea, Lord: I have believed that thou art the Christ, the Son
of God, even he that cometh into the world" (v. 27). The conviction of these two was the result of their having been in His
presence and having beheld the evidence.

12. The disciples at supper

The eleven disciples who were privileged to eat the last supper
with Jesus had been with Him for about three years. During this
time they had beheld His works and heard His teaching. After they
had eaten, Jesus began to prepare them for His going away and for
the work to which He was sending them. Following the discourse
(chs. 14-16), which abounded in words of comfort, assurance,
instruction, and promise, the testimony of the disciples was, "Now
know we that thou knowest all things, and needest not that any
man should ask thee: by this we believe that thou camest forth
from God" (16:30). The evidence on which this belief rested was
the fulness and completeness of His knowledge revealed in His
teaching. They had had ample opportunity to examine this teaching.

13. Pilate

The testimony of Pilate is that of a Roman ruler, whose conclusion should have been reached after a calm and impartial hearing

of the evidence presented. Having listened to the testimony of the Jewish rulers, Pilate then examined Jesus. The testimony of Jesus that He was a king, but not of a kingdom of this world, so assured Pilate that his verdict was, "I find no crime in him" (18:38). This should have been sufficient for the release of Jesus, but Pilate weakened before the Jews.

After scourging Jesus and allowing his soldiers to mock Him, the Roman pontiff again came to the Jews with the same conclusion, "I find no crime in him" (19:4). Next, having arrayed Jesus in the mock apparel of a king, Pilate presented Him to the Jewish mob in the hope that they would retract their demand for His death. However, they only cried louder, "Crucify him, crucify him!" Pilate's reply was, "Take him yourselves, and crucify him"; and for the third time affirmed, "I find no crime in him" (19:6). To the everlasting shame of Pilate and as a travesty on fair government, Pilate lacked the character to defend the thrice-acclaimed conviction, "I find no crime in him," and allowed the will of the mob to prevail. But his witness as a Roman ruler to the character of Jesus shall stand as long as time endures. He found *no* crime in Him.

14. Thomas

Except for his own, John seems to reserve the testimony of Thomas to the last. Jewish testimony reached its climax when Thomas acknowledged Jesus as Lord and God. Thomas is introduced first as a pessimist, yet one possessing the courage to die with Him whom he had determined to follow. When Jesus had indicated that He was going to Bethany, near Jerusalem, where the Jews had so recently sought His life, Thomas said, "Let us also go, that we may die with him" (11:16). He is presented next as being uncertain of Jesus' teaching and somewhat impatient with the things his teacher was saying, when he says, "Lord, we know not whither thou goest; how know we the way?" (14:5). Even after the resurrection of Jesus, Thomas manifested a very skeptical attitude. He was absent when Jesus appeared to the disciples on the day of His resurrection, and when told by the others, "We have seen the Lord," he had replied, "Except I shall see in his hands the print of the nails, and put my finger into the print of the nails, and put my hand into his side, I will not believe" (20:25).

But what is the final testimony of this pessimistic, uncertain skeptic? His final testimony is the greatest that could be borne by any Jew, for it is either truth, based on evidence, or it is blasphemy. When he saw Jesus and the Lord urged him to fulfill his expressed desire to put his finger and hand into the wounds, his confident answer was "My Lord and my God" (20:28). No testimony to faith could be stronger than was his.

15. The writer

The concluding testimony is that of the writer of the book. Much has been written on the question of the authorship of the Gospel of John. It does not come within the scope of this work to discuss the subject. Suffice it to say that the book is here; therefore, it was written by someone. What is in it is fact or fiction. If fact, the evidence must sustain it; if not, the evidence cannot sustain it. Herein are offered the claims and testimony to sustain the claims so that each may come to his own conclusion on the basis of the weight of the testimony.

When Jesus was crucified, one of the soldiers pierced His side, "and straightway there came out blood and water. And he that hath seen hath borne witness, and his witness is true: and he knoweth that he saith true, that ye also may believe" (19:34, 35). This is the simple testimony of an eyewitness.

After Peter's question had been answered concerning John, John added his final word, "This is the disciple that beareth witness of these things" (21:24a). To this testimony others who had known the writer for a long time added their testimony saying, "and we know that his witness is true" (v. 24b).

Summary

The witness of both enemies and friends who had seen Him, heard Him, and had opportunity to observe and form a judgment on this basis, was that He is the Messiah, the theme of Moses and the prophets, the Son of God, the King of Israel. He was a teacher come from God, the Savior of the world, the holy one of God. Enemies admitted the signs that the world was gone after Him and that they could do nothing to stop the movement. Others said that never man spoke as did He, that He was a prophet, a worshiper of

God, the Son of God. Women testified that He could have averted death, that He was able to raise the dead, that He was the Christ, the Son of God. By her silence Mary gave testimony to His claim to be the Son of God. Others believed, on the strength of His teaching, that He came from God. Pilate could find no crime in Him, and Thomas was convinced that He was Lord and God. The writer bears his testimony that the things he has written are true.

As said in the introduction to this chapter, the testimony of these expresses only the impression made on those who saw and heard Jesus. The testimony is from friends and enemies, from the indifferent and the concerned. It is from men and women of all walks of life. Was John able to create the character of Jesus and then put such words of testimony into the mouths of witnesses? Or, did Jesus live and these bear such testimony to His impression on them? Reason's function is to weigh the matter and to formulate a judgment compatible with the weight of the testimony.

John's purpose in writing his Gospel was that man might believe that Jesus is the Christ, and through that faith have eternal life. Since all belief rests on evidence, John has presented testimony which he believes will beget and sustain faith. As said above, his Gospel is not a biography of the life of Christ. Instead of writing one, John selects from the approximate one thousand days of Jesus' ministry incidents and teaching from about twenty of those days which he offers as evidence to prove his proposition.

The Father's Testimony —Through Works

6

Immediately following the healing of the lame man at the pool of Bethesda (5:2-9), the Jews charged Jesus with breaking the sabbath and with making Himself equal with God. Jesus startled the Jews by responding with the most sweeping claim in reference to His work and responsibility found in the Gospel.

First, He said He could do nothing of Himself, but only what He had seen the Father doing (5:19); "and greater works than these will he show him, that ye may marvel" (v. 20). Jesus proceeded with a general statement showing what the "greater works" would be, "For as the Father raiseth the dead and giveth them life, even so the Son also giveth life to whom he will" (v. 21). These "greater works" would include the raising of both the physical and spiritual dead and the giving of both physical and spiritual life. Jesus followed this broad statement with three specific works the Father was giving Him to do:

(1) Judgment was now given into the hand of the Son that all should honor the Son as they honor the Father. Refusing to honor the Son is refusing to honor the Father (vv. 22-23). This claim was an admission to their charge that He acknowledged equality with

the Father (v. 18); but also it was an assertion that the equality proceeded from the Father and not from a presumptuous claim of His own. His words, works, and life would verify this claim and thereby bring into judgment all who reject Him. The claim also further identified Him with the messianic promise.

(2) The second claim made by Jesus was that as the Father had eternal life in Himself, so had He given to the Son also to have life in Himself, which life would be imparted by the word of the Son. He further claimed that the hour had now come when men should hear the voice of the Son and possess that life (vv. 24-27). This claim pertained to spiritual life and Jesus' power to raise to that life from the state of spiritual death.

(3) The third of the claims made was an enlargement or further explanation of the general claim, "For as the Father raiseth the dead and giveth them life, even so the Son also giveth life to whom he will" (v. 21). They were not to be astounded at the thought of His giving spiritual life through Himself, for "the hour cometh (future), in which all that are in the tombs shall hear his voice, and shall come forth; they that have done good, unto the resurrection of life; and they that have done evil, unto the resurrection of judgment" (vv. 28-29).

In summary, the three claims show that all judgment, present and future, is now in the hand of the Son; decisions of judgment are to be made by Him. The final judgment will be determined by His word (12:48-50). The responsibility of giving spiritual life and of raising men from death in sin is now His and is to be effected by His word. And finally, the raising of all the physically dead, the righteous and the wicked, is committed to Him and likewise will be accomplished by His word. These claims definitely relate Him to the Father as equal with Him; His word was the Father's word, to which they should now give heed as unto the Father.

Without waiting for the Jews to recover from the stun of these declarations, Jesus hastened to affirm that the Father would bear witness to the truthfulness of these claims. He told them how they had sent unto John the immerser, who had borne testimony to the truth that he (John) was not the Christ, but that Jesus was from God. "But," Jesus continued, "the witness which I have is greater than that of John; for the works which the Father hath given me to accomplish, the very works that I do, bear witness of me, that the Father hath sent me. And the Father that sent me, he hath borne witness of me" (5:36, 37). Having told them in the preceding conversation that the works were divine, Jesus now tells them that through these works the Father bears witness to His claims. The Father's testimony would be through miraculous works which He would do; these would be the confirmation of the claim that the Father had sent Him. The Father's testimony would be threefold: (1) the works, (2) Scripture, and (3) the raising of Jesus from the dead.

There can be no question that John included the "signs"—special miracles of Jesus—as "works" of God. In referring to the miracle of healing the lame man at the pool of Bethesda, Jesus said, "I did one work, and ye all marvel because thereof" (7:21). He then asked, in reference to the healing of the lame man, "are ye wroth with me, because I made a man every whit whole on the sabbath?" (v. 23). The "work" was the making of the lame man whole. He later testified, "the works that I do in my Father's name, these bear witness of me" (10:25), and challenged His enemies, "If I do not the works of my Father, believe me not. But if I do them, though ye believe not me, believe the works: that ye may know and understand that the Father is in me, and I in the Father" (vv. 37, 38). The purpose of the works was to save life and to confirm His claim of relation to the Father as the Son of God, that through belief in Him they might be saved.

Definition of Terms

Three words, *signs, wonders,* and *powers,* are used in the Scripture to designate the miracle and its purpose, effect, and source. Therefore, it is profitable to define these words and to point out the ones used by John. A fourth word, which of itself has no relation to the miraculous but is used by John to designate the miracles of Jesus, is *work* or *works*. To John, Christ's signs are simply "works of God," acts in harmony with His deity and the purpose for which He came into the world.

1. Sign

The word used by John throughout the Gospel, except for one occasion when he quotes Jesus, is *sēmion,* "1. a sign, mark, token . . . 2. a sign, prodigy, portent. b. of miracles and wonders by which God authenticates the men sent by him, or by which men prove that the cause they are pleading is God's" (Thayer). "It verifies claims and communications" and "discloses the very nature and purpose of God."[1] Of all the miracles done by Jesus, John selects seven which he weaves into his Gospel as signs, which testify to Christ's deity, and establish John's proposition that Jesus is the Christ.

2. Wonder

Although Luke does not use the word *wonder* in his Gospel, in Acts he uses the word more times than it is used in the rest of the New Testament writings. The word *teras* is defined as "a prodigy, portent; miracle performed by any one; in the N.T. it is found only in the plural and joined with *semeia*" (Thayer). John himself never uses the word, but does quote Jesus one time as having used it: "Except ye see signs and wonders, ye will in no wise believe" (4:48).

3. Power

Power, from *dunamis,* indicates "strength, ability, power; a. universally inherent power, power residing in a thing by virtue of its nature, or which a person or thing exerts and puts forth. . . . b. specifically, the power of performing miracles" (Thayer). This points to the divine energy exerted in its act. John does not use this word at all; instead, he uses the term *work*. To him, such power is a normal "work" in the mission of one such as Jesus.

4. Work or works

John's companion word to *sign* is *work* or *works, ergon,* "3. an act, deed, thing done. Of sundry or signal acts of Christ to rouse men to believe in him and to accomplish their salvation" (Thayer). As suggested above, John considers Christ's signs simply "works of God." What Jesus did were "works which the Father hath given me to accomplish" (5:36). The healing of the lame man was only "one work" which He had done (7:21); He was doing the works

---

1. Baker's *Dictionary of Theology*, p. 356.

which the Father had sent Him to do (9:4). His challenge was, "Many good works have I showed you from the Father; for which of those works do ye stone me?" (10:32). His claim was, "The Father abiding in me doeth his works" (14:10).

Trench sums up the difference in the several words as follows: "In the name *wonder,* the astonishment, which the work produces upon the beholders . . . is transferred to the work itself . . . But the miracle is not a *'wonder'* only; it is also a *sign,* a token and indication of the near presence and working of God . . . Frequently, also the miracles are styled *'powers'* or *'mighty works,'* that is, of God. As in the term 'wonder,' or 'miracle,' the effect is transferred and gives a name to the cause, so here the cause gives its name to the effect."[2] Vine's comment is, "A sign is intended to appeal to the understanding, a wonder appeals to the imagination, a power (*dunamis*) indicates its source as supernatural."[3] See also Baker's *Dictionary of Theology,* pp. 356ff.

Witness to the Signs

An interesting fact that adds weight to the testimony of miracles is that the enemies of Jesus never denied the miracles; however, they refused to accept them as being performed by divine power. Effort was never made by the Lord or by His disciples to prove that a miracle had been accomplished. The miracles were recognized and accepted by all; they spoke for themselves.

1. The signs in general

When Nicodemus came to Jesus by night, it was because he was impressed by what Jesus was teaching and by the signs He was offering to verify the teaching. His testimony was, "Rabbi, we know that thou art a teacher come from God; for no one can do these signs that thou doest, except God be with him" (3:2). He did not question the authenticity of the signs.

The testimony of the multitude was, "When the Christ shall come, will he do more signs than those which this man hath done?" (7:31).

---

2. Richard Chenevix Trench, *Notes on the Miracles of Our Lord,* pp. 1-5.

3. W. E. Vine, Vol. IV, p. 228.

The Pharisees likewise bare witness to the signs in general when they said, "What do we? for this man doeth many signs" (11:47). No one from among all the various classes of the Jews debated the existence of the miracles; they recognized them as such and testified to the fact.

2. The sign of the man born blind

The restoring of sight by Jesus to the man born blind aroused a great stir among the Jews because it was done on the sabbath. The sign itself is abundantly attested. The neighbors were astounded and asked, "How then were thine eyes opened?" (9:10). The parents of the man testified, "We know that this is our son, and that he was born blind: but how he now seeth, we know not; or who opened his eyes, we know not: ask him; he is of age" (9:20-21). The charge of the Pharisees of the judicial court was that Jesus was a sinner because He kept not the sabbath. The response of others becomes their witness to the fact of the sign when they ask, "How can a man that is a sinner do such signs?" (9:16). Likewise, the testimony of the Jews of the city took the form of a question, "Can a demon open the eyes of the blind?" (10:21; see also 11:37). And finally, there is the witness of the man himself, who testified that Jesus had anointed his eyes and told him to go and wash in the pool of Siloam. He did this and received his sight (9:11, 15). And further, he affirmed, "that, whereas I was blind, now I see" (vv. 25, 30).

The reality of factuality of the miracle was not under question. The question concerned how it was done and what the character was of one who would do such a work on the sabbath. These were paramount with the Pharisees. The neighbors were curious; the parents were afraid; the Pharisees were designing; the man was positive. But all bare witness to the fact of the sign.

3. The raising of Lazarus from the dead

The final miracle of Jesus recorded by John, and intended by him to be the climax of them all, was the occasion at which the Pharisees determined to put Him to death. The Pharisees themselves are the witnesses to the factuality of the miracle. They were deeply concerned as to what they should do in the presence of such works by one who claimed to be from God; therefore, they called a council to determine their procedure. Their question was, "What do we? for this man doeth many signs. If we let him thus alone, all men will believe on him" (11:47, 48). The signs had them at bay; they were now on the defensive but must take the offensive if they were not to be defeated. They determined to put Him to death (11:53).

Shortly after this determination to put Him to death, Jesus entered the city amidst the shouts of the multitude, "Hosanna: Blessed is he that cometh in the name of the Lord, even the King of Israel" (12:13). Much of this enthusiasm had been excited by the raising of Lazarus (v. 18); and again the Pharisees were exceedingly perplexed. Their concern over the results of the raising of Lazarus and their determination to put Him to death is testimony to the fact that Lazarus was raised from the dead. Their testimony was, "Behold how ye prevail nothing; lo, the world is gone after him" (12:19).

There was no question raised by any as to the signs themselves; the testimony of all was that the signs were factual. The real point was that they refused to accept that to which the sign pointed and testified: the deity of Jesus—the fact that the Messiah was among them. But He was not the Messiah of their expectations; therefore, they refused to deal fairly with the signs themselves.

The Signs

In a movement such as that undertaken by Jesus, in which the Father of man and the Creator of the *Kosmos* were revealing themselves, it is only reasonable to expect the miraculous. Isolated and unrelated miracles are always to be received with suspicion. Those of Jesus are neither isolated nor unrelated but are identified with a great historical movement which fulfills a plan that originated in eternity, began to be revealed in Eden (Gen. 3:15), and continued with the promise of God to Abraham. This promise to Abraham had continued in its development for nearly two *millenia.*

Miracles are not to be considered as acts in contradiction to laws of nature, but as the intervention of a law higher than those ordinarily working in that particular realm. This writing does not propose to spend time in an effort to establish the possibility, credibility, or probability of miracles. The signs will be presented as John presented them, as works of God which were in harmony with the character and mission of Jesus and which related Him to God. His miracles carried with them qualities of moral value.

John affirms that Jesus had done many other signs not written in his Gospel, but that "these are written, that ye may believe that Jesus is the Christ, the Son of God; and that believing ye may have life in his name" (20:30-31). As John presents miracles as signs, they establish the grand fact that Jesus had authority and power over all realms; He possessed power which belonged to God Himself. Thus these related Him and His work to God.

Miracles were direct evidence to His claims as Savior, shepherd, and sustainer of man and his needs. They substantiate the claims that He came from God, was one with God, and came to reveal God. The miracles as recorded by John sustain a moral relation to His teaching. Apart from the resurrection and the draft of fishes after the resurrection, there are seven signs presented by the writer of this Gospel. The resurrection will be dealt with as separate testimony to Christ's deity.

1. Turning water to wine (2:1-11)

The beginning of Jesus' signs was turning water to wine at the wedding feast in Cana of Galilee. John spends no time on incidents of the wedding which might be of passing interest, such as who were the bride and groom, who were present, what was the relation of Jesus to the couple, or why the supply of wine was insufficient. With John the central figure was Jesus and the important incident was the sign. Jesus instructed the servants to fill six waterpots with water, each containing between eighteen and twenty-seven gallons. The servants were instructed to draw out from the jars; and when this was done, the wine was found to be superior in quality to that served earlier in the feast. The disciples beheld the miracle and believed.

This sign demonstrated that Jesus is the Lord of creation. He who created the vine through which the water must pass to form the grape that becomes wine and He who could turn the water directly into wine apart from the vine are one. In this sign He demonstrated that He is the master of matter; when He wills, it obeys. Also, He is the Lord of quality (Tenney); the wine which He provided was superior to that provided by the host.

2. Healing the nobleman's son (4:46-54)

Upon His return from Jerusalem to Galilee, Jesus found there a certain Capernaum nobleman whose son was ill. At the word of Jesus, "Go thy way; thy son liveth," the man believed and started on his way. It was discovered later by the nobleman that at the hour Jesus had spoken the son was made well. The distance from Cana to Capernaum was sixteen miles. Jesus here not only demonstrated His power over disease and the forces of the body's destruction, but also He showed Himself to be master of distance and space. These are no barriers to Him who claimed to come from God.

3. Healing the lame man (5:1-9)

It was in Jerusalem at the pool of Bethesda that Jesus gave the next sign mentioned by John. This miracle was enacted upon a man who for thirty-eight years had been in his infirmity. No doubt it was a pathetic sight to behold one who for so long had been in this condition, lying helplessly by the pool, living under the delusion that if someone could be there to put him in the pool at a certain time he would be healed. At the simple words of Jesus, "Arise, take up thy bed, and walk," the man straightway was made whole and took up his bed and did as he had been instructed.

In this sign Jesus proved Himself to be the master of time. Whether thirty-eight minutes or thirty-eight years, the time made no difference. Jesus is the master of time. He is Lord of truth; the vast distance between the emptiness of tradition that said agitated water had the ability to heal and the reality of truth is demonstrated. The truth made him free from that which tradition had failed to touch.

4. Feeding the five thousand (6:1-14)

From Jerusalem Jesus retraced His steps to Galilee. From there He crossed the Jordan to the northeast shore of Lake Tiberias. Multitudes were thronging after Him. After teaching them He had them be seated, and with five small loaves and two fishes, a lad's lunch, Jesus fed five thousand men, besides women and children who may have been in the crowd.

In this sign Jesus demonstrated His claim to provide for man's physical needs, and by analogy, to provide for his spiritual needs. Likewise, He demonstrated that He is the Lord of quantity. From a few grains one might eventually grow enough wheat to feed such a throng. But the Maker of the original wheat grains could cut through the process of time and rain and sunshine, and in a moment produce the quantity necessary to the need.

5. Jesus' walking on the sea (6:16-21)

The crowd had been dismissed and the disciples were returning across the sea in a boat. Jesus had retired to the mountain that He might be alone. Late in the night as the disciples were in the midst of the sea, a storm rose on the little body of water. The hour was a fearsome one. In such an hour and time of need, Jesus came to them, walking upon the sea and drawing near. At first they were frightened by His appearance; but at His word, "It is I; be not afraid," they received Him into the boat.

John makes no mention of His stilling the tempest, but tells only of His coming to them, walking on the water. By this act He showed Himself to be the master of the natural forces of wind and wave and the Lord of gravity and its power. Also by this manifestation of Himself, He demonstrated His concern for His own when the winds are contrary and they are alone in the midst of the storm. He would have them know that He is present in time of need and that in His hand lies the control of all forces in the natural world.

6. Restoring sight to the man born blind (9:1-12)

Once again we find Jesus in the city of Jerusalem. In His discourse with the Jews of the city, Jesus made the claim, "I am the light of the world" (8:12). Passing by He beheld a man born blind; He placed clay on his eyes and told him to go and wash in the pool of Siloam. As has been pointed out, the miracle aroused the city because of the day on which it occurred.

In this remarkable sign Jesus revealed Himself as the master of light, exercising control over the power of darkness. His claim to be the light of the world stood confirmed. Likewise, He was and is the master over adversity; He can turn one's darkness into light and make each forget the long years of darkness in which he had walked.

7. Raising of Lazarus (11:39-44)

Early in His ministry in Jerusalem, Jesus had claimed the power to give life; He had said that to this the Father would bear witness (ch. 5). The raising of Lazarus from the dead was the sign that climaxed all other signs and gave indisputable proof to the claim. Standing before the tomb of His friend who had died, Jesus cried with a loud voice, "Lazarus, come forth." Immediately the living body of the one recently deceased came forth.

Jesus had now confirmed His claim to be able to raise the dead and His claim that He is the resurrection and the life. He had proved Himself to be the master over death and the giver of life. In this sign He has given His personal guarantee that every body now lying in the tomb will at some time hear His voice and come forth.

One may contend, "But no one today has seen one of the signs!" and this is correct. Signs pertained to the age of the introduction of Jesus and the inauguration of His kingdom. The weight of their testimony to us is in the moral character of the signs. In each of them, there is a relation between the sign and the teaching of Jesus. Someone has said, "The miracles are not the mere proofs of a revelation; they are themselves the revelation."[4] They reveal the deity of Him who walked among men. They are the Father's testimony to the claims of His Son that He and His message are from God.

---

4. H. Wace, "Miracles," *ISBE*, Vol. III, p. 2064.

The Father's Testimony —Through Scripture

7

One of the unique characteristics of the Bible and the religion that it reveals, one that distinguishes it from all other religions, is its element of prophecy. It records history before it happens. The true prophets of both Old and New Testaments acted as spokesmen for God. God through them was revealing the past, dealing with the present, and foretelling events of the future. Writers of the Old Testament foretold the history of heathen nations, of Judah and Israel, and of the coming of one in whom the purpose of God would be completely fulfilled. The force of the argument from prophecy may be summarized as follows:

1. Man unaided cannot foretell events of history or the coming and actions of an individual. Only a supernatural power can do this.

2. The Bible does foretell certain events that were to come, and it also foretells the coming and actions of individuals.

3. Therefore, the Bible is not of man, but is supernatural in its origin and teaching.

In this statement of the proposition, the major premise will be granted, or at least it is assumed that it will be granted; that is, that man unaided by the supernatural cannot foretell history. The minor premise, that is, that the Bible foretells persons and events to come, will have to be proved. But if the minor premise is proved to the satisfaction of him who investigates, the conclusion will inevitably follow that the Bible is not of man but is of supernatural origin. Jesus appealed to Scripture as the witness of God to His claims. Luke recorded His conversation held with the disciples after His resurrection, in which He said, "These are my words which I spake unto you, while I was yet with you, that all things must needs be fulfilled, which are written in the *law of Moses,* and *the prophets,* and *the psalms,* concerning me" (Luke 24:44). We may look in these three sections of the Old Covenant writings for prophecies that point to Him.

This evidence for His claim to deity is not overlooked by John in his Gospel but is constantly appealed to and emphasized both by Jesus and by the apostles. In defense of His claim to judge, raise the dead, and give life (5:19-29), Jesus affirmed that He had greater witness than that of John the Baptist. The Father was bearing witness through the works which He had given Him to do (5:36-37). Jesus then appealed to a second testimony of the Father when He said, "Ye search the scriptures, because ye think that in them ye have eternal life; and these are they which bear witness of me; and ye will not come to me, that ye may have life" (5:39-40). The life was not in Scripture, but in the "me" to whom Scripture testified. In this statement Jesus does not limit Scripture to any particular part, but includes the whole, including Moses, the prophets, and the psalms, as claimed by Him in the record of Luke.

Before considering testimony of Scripture as presented in the Gospel of John, it is profitable to look at Jesus' attitude toward the whole of the Old Testament writings. The word of Jesus, which is probably the most significant revelation of His feeling for the body of Scripture, is found in His reply to the Jews when He said, "Is it not written in your law, I said, Ye are gods? If he called them gods, unto whom the word of God came (and the scripture cannot be broken) . . ." (10:34-35). In this statement Jesus recognized two definite principles: (1) the Scripture, "your law," i.e., the law given to you and to which you appeal, is the word of God; and (2) Scripture cannot be broken. In this Jesus recognizes that the written word of the Old Testament is from God. It is inspired, because it is of God and "came" to them; they did not discover it. It is infallible and indestructible, because "it cannot be broken"; it cannot be denied or set aside and is therefore permanent or fixed until He who gave it sees fit to change it.

This attitude toward Scripture is maintained by Jesus throughout His ministry. God was bearing witness of Him through Scripture; therefore, Scripture is the word of God (5:38). From within the believer would flow rivers of living waters, "as the scripture hath said" (7:38). The betrayal by Judas, by which he would be lost, would fulfill the prophecy of Scripture (13:18; 17:12). At this point there was never a question or doubt in the mind of Jesus; His whole life and work was predetermined and foretold by the Father. Scripture had declared it; what He was doing was fulfilling what they had declared. Men might break themselves against the law, but Scripture itself could not be broken.

The testimony of Scripture must not be sought for in only a few passages quoted from the Old Testament, but it should be recognized in the entire hope of the Old Covenant and must be seen in Jesus as He fulfills that hope. It was of this that Jesus spoke when He said, "all things must needs be fulfilled, which are written in the law of Moses, and the prophets, and the psalms, concerning me" (Luke 24:44). This thought was also in the mind of Philip when he said to Nathanael, "We have found him, of whom Moses in the law, and the prophets, wrote, Jesus of Nazareth" (1:45).

The Writings of Moses

In refuting further the charge of the Jews that He was worthy of death because He had healed a man on the sabbath, Jesus said, "Think not that I will accuse you to the Father: there is one that accuseth you, even Moses, on whom ye have set your hope. For if ye believed Moses, ye would believe me; for *he wrote of me*. But if ye believe not his writings, how shall ye believe my words?" (5:45-47). In this Jesus did not limit Moses to any one passage or section of his writings; Moses had written of Jesus.

1. The seed of the woman (Gen. 3:15)

From the beginning Moses had in view one to come. This one was to have been the "seed" of the woman, with a definite mission. As written by Moses, God had said, "And I will put enmity between thee (the serpent) and the woman, and between thy seed and her seed: he (the seed of the woman) shall bruise thy head, and thou (the serpent) shalt bruise his heel" (Gen. 3:15). The theme of this promise runs throughout the Old Covenant; it is the hope of one to come who would crush the power of Satan, but who, in so doing, would suffer the equivalent of a bruised heel.

The thought of this conflict is in the forefront throughout the Book of John. The book is a book of conflicts: the conflict between light and darkness, truth and error, right and wrong, good and evil, belief and unbelief, life and death, and friends and foes. In its finality, it was the conflict between God and Satan. This is the conflict foretold by Moses.

Jesus indicated that He was not born of natural generation when He said, "Ye are from beneath; I am from above: ye are of this world; I am not of this world" (8:23). In the conversation that followed, Jesus told the Jews who had believed on Him that if they would abide in His word, they should know the truth and that through the truth they would be made free. To this they retorted, "We are Abraham's seed, and have never yet been in bondage to any man: How sayest thou, Ye shall be made free?" (8:31-33). Jesus' reply was that everyone who commits sin is the bondservant of sin. "And the bondservant abideth not in the house for ever: the son abideth for ever. If therefore the Son shall make you free, ye shall be free indeed" (vv. 34-36). The first claim (v. 23) relates Jesus to one born not of natural generation but sent from above; the second identifies Satan as the one who brings men into bondage; the third identifies Himself as the one who should make men free.

The debate between Jesus and these Jews did not end at this point. Jesus proceeded to identify Himself with the Father and to deny their relation to either God or Abraham, whom they claimed as their father; but rather He identified them with the family of the devil. "I speak the things which I have seen with my Father: and ye also do the things which ye heard from your father" (8:38). Immediately they claimed Abraham as their father; to this claim Jesus replied that if Abraham were their father they would do the works of Abraham. Instead, they sought to kill Him, Jesus, a man who told them the truth, which Abraham would not be doing. Angered at this, they then claimed that God was their

Father; to this Jesus replied that if God were their Father they would love Him whom the Father had sent: "For I came forth and am come from God; for neither have I come of myself, but he sent me" (v. 42). Jesus followed this with the charge in which the conversation reached its climax, "Ye are of your father the devil, and the lusts of your father it is your will to do. He was a murderer from the beginning, and standeth not in the truth, because there is no truth in him. When he speaketh a lie, he speaketh of his own: for he is a liar, and the father thereof" (8:44).

As the time drew near for Jesus to meet His death, He said to the disciples, "The hour is come, that the Son of man should be glorified" (12:23); He followed this with the claim, "Now is the judgment of this world: now shall the prince of this world be cast out" (12:31). In putting Jesus to death, the world of ungodly and evil men was only judging and condemning itself. In Christ's death, which appeared to the world to be His defeat, Satan was cast down from that pinnacle of rule which he had held so long—the rule over the human family and of death. A few moments later Jesus said, "For the prince of the world cometh: and he hath nothing in me" (14:30). And finally, as if it were already accomplished, Jesus said that the Holy Spirit would convict the world of judgment, "because the prince of this world hath been judged" (16:11).

Satan's power over man has never been the same since Jesus came. In the conflict with him, Jesus bruised his head as He crushed his power; but as He accomplished this mighty feat His "heel was bruised." That is, in the comparison, His death was as the bruising of the heel in crushing the head of the serpent. Truly, Moses wrote of Him when he wrote of "the seed of the woman" who should bruise the head of the great serpent. If the Jews had been spiritually alert, they would have seen in Jesus and in His work Him of whom Moses wrote.

2. The seed of Abraham (Gen. 12:1-3)

It was of Him that Moses wrote when he recorded God's promise to Abraham, "And in thee shall all the families of the earth be blessed" (Gen. 12:3); and again, "And in thy seed shall all the nations of the earth be blessed" (Gen. 22:18). This one, through whom families and nations of the earth should be blessed, was the central theme of both Moses and the prophets.

In His debate with the Jews, Jesus denied that in their behavior the Jews were children either of Abraham or of God, saying, "Your father Abraham rejoiced to see my day; and he saw it, and was glad" (8:56). This identified Him with the seed of Abraham. Abraham saw His day in the birth of Isaac, the child of promise (Gen. 21:1-7); he saw it in the casting out of Ishmael, "for in Isaac shall thy seed be called" (Gen. 21:12); he saw it in the offering of Isaac on Mount Moriah, in which, in a figure, he received him back from the dead and called the place Jehovah-jireh—Jehovah will provide (Gen. 22).

The promise to Abraham was finding fulfillment in the "whosoever" of John 3:16, which would include all families and all nations of earth. These families and nations were included when Jesus said, "And other sheep I have which are not of this fold: them also I must bring, and they shall hear my voice; and they shall become one flock, one shepherd" (10:16). The "other sheep" would be the Gentiles, those from all families and nations.

When certain Gentiles came to the feast and made request of Philip, "Sir, we would see Jesus" (12:21), Philip found Andrew, and the two brought the request to Jesus. It was then that Jesus declared His hour had come and that the prince of this world was being cast out. He then continued, "And I, if I be lifted up from the earth, will draw all men unto myself" (12:32). In this He was signifying what manner of death He should die, and declaring that His death on the cross would become the drawing power for all men, Jews and Gentiles. It was too late for the Gentiles to be included in His earthly ministry, and it was too early for the fulfillment of the promise to Abraham that in his seed all nations should be blessed. But in His death the promise would be fulfilled, and men of all families and of all nations would have the opportunity to be blessed through their coming to Him. Again, the Father had borne witness of Him through that which Moses had written of Him.

3. The heavenly ladder (Gen. 28:12)

The enmity between Jacob and his brother Esau forced Jacob to flee into the land of Padan-aram. Night overtook him in the neighborhood of Bethel, where, as he slept, "he dreamed; and, behold, a ladder set up on the earth, and the top of it reached to heaven; and, behold, the angels of God ascending and descending on it" (Gen. 28:12). At the head of the ladder stood Jehovah, who renewed the promise made to Abraham that He would give to His seed the land on which Jacob slept and would make of him a great nation. This was followed with the spiritual promise, "And in thy seed shall all the families of the earth be blessed" (v. 14).

Early in His ministry Jesus identified Himself with this dream and thus with its promise. At the declaration of Nathanael's faith in Jesus, "Rabbi, thou art the Son of God; thou art King of Israel" (1:49), Jesus assured him that because of his faith through that which Jesus had just said to him he would see greater things than these. He then said to Nathanael and Philip, "Ye shall see the heaven opened, and the angels of God ascending and descending upon the Son of man" (1:51). By this Jesus identified Himself as the ladder of the dream on which the message from God to man, and the messages from man to God, would descend and ascend. This also identified Him with the promised seed in whom all the families of the earth should be blessed. Again, "Moses wrote of me."

4. The prophet (Deut. 18:15-18)

At Mount Sinai Jehovah had spoken to the people directly. When the people heard the thundering voice out of the midst of the fire, the cloud and the thick darkness, felt the trembling of the earth, and heard the thunder of the lightning, they were fearful and trembled. They came to Moses with the request that Jehovah not speak to them directly but that He speak to Moses and let Moses speak to them. Jehovah heard and granted the request; no more would He speak to them directly.

Later, as Moses was preparing the people for their entrance into the land of Canaan, Jehovah warned them that none among them should practice any form of divination or sorcery as practiced by the nations, nor should they seek information from any such source (Deut. 18:9-14). Instead of receiving information from heathen practices of divination or sorcery and instead of having words spoken directly by Jehovah, they would receive information from God through prophets whom He would raise up. He assured them that He would raise them up a prophet from among the people like unto Moses and put His words in the prophet's mouth. The prophet would be under obligation to speak unto them all things that God should command him. Further, it would come to pass that whosoever refused to listen to God's words which that prophet spoke would be answerable to God (Deut. 18:18-19). (See Chap. 3). From that time God spoke to His people through prophets whom He raised up, in whose mouth He put His words, "For no prophecy ever came by the will of man: but men spake from God, being moved by the Holy Spirit" (II Peter 1:21).

According to the Gospel of John, Jesus fulfilled every principle of the prophet as set forth by Moses. He did nothing of Himself, but did that which He had seen the Father doing (5:19). He claimed, "My teaching is not mine, but his that sent me" (7:16); "I do nothing of myself, but as the Father taught me, I speak these things" (8:28); "For I spake not from myself; but the Father that sent me, he hath given me a commandment, what I should say, and what I should speak . . . the things therefore which I speak, even as the Father hath said unto me, so I speak" (12:49. See also 14:10).

God raised Him from among His brethren; God sent Him; God gave Him the words He should speak; and God would judge by His word any who should reject Christ and His teaching (7:24; 12:48). Truly Moses wrote of Him, for in Him was fulfilled in every respect the ideal of the prophet who should speak the words of God. The revelation by the prophets of the Old Covenant had met the needs of the hour and had pointed the people to a Messiah and kingdom to come, but in Jesus truth and grace found their completeness, fulness and finality for all men (1:16-18).

5. Types and shadows

Moses also wrote of Him in the feasts and sacrifices of the law, for herein were types that would be fulfilled in one to come. Had the Jews understood the writings of Moses, they would have seen in Jesus the realization of that to which the types pointed. Surely to the pious and thinking Jew there must have been more to the lambs eaten and the animals sacrificed than something physical and material. Animal sacrifices could not take away sin, else would they have ceased to be offered; and yet, year by year sins were remembered and sacrifices were offered (Heb. 10:1-4).

As the people of Israel prepared to leave Egypt, they kept the first of their festivals, the Passover. In this feast the lamb was slain and prepared for the family, and the blood was sprinkled on the doorposts that the destroyer might pass over the family of that house. In preparing and eating the lamb, not a bone of the sacrifice should be broken (Exod. 12:46; Num. 9:12). True, when Jesus said to the Jews, "Moses wrote of me" (John 5), it was too early for them to realize the true significance of the Passover at that time. But as Jesus was offered on the cross and not a bone of Him was broken as they pierced the side, "that the scripture might be fulfilled, A bone of him shall not be broken" (19:36), they should have seen in Him the fulfillment of the type and should have recognized in Him the realization of their hope. The type was now fulfilled in the substance; Moses had written of Him and the thing written was now accomplished.

At Mount Sinai God gave Moses a system of sacrifices and offerings which were usually spoken of as the Levitical sacrifices because of the priests' functions in these offerings. These sacrifices of bulls and goats, of lambs and heifers, of pigeons and turtledoves could never of themselves take away sin. The psalmist revealed that the more spiritual among them were fully conscious of this, saying, "Sacrifice and offering thou hast no delight in; Mine ears hast thou opened: Burnt-offering and sin-offering hast thou not required. Then said I, Lo, I am come; In the roll of the book it is written of me: I delight to do thy will, O my God; Yea, thy law is within my heart. I have proclaimed glad tidings of righteousness in the great assembly; Lo, I will not refrain my lips, O Jehovah, thou knowest" (Ps. 40:6-9). In the law God had required righteousness, and in the sacrifices He had made provision for the hope of ultimate redemption for all who should sin against that standard of righteousness. Now came John the Baptist saying, "Behold, the Lamb of God, that taketh away the sin of the world!" (1:29); and again, "Behold, the Lamb of God!" (1:36). Philip saw in Him the realization of Moses' writings when he said, "We have found him, of whom Moses in the law, and the prophets, wrote" (1:45).

The wilderness wandering of the Israelites was fraught with many temptations. Seemingly, the greatest of these temptations was discontentment with God's provisions for their welfare; continually they murmured against Him. The journey was almost over for them; they neared the border of Edom, where once more they yielded to the temptation to murmur and complain against

God because of their discouragement. They regretted having left
Egypt and now loathed the manna that God had provided for
them. As a result of their murmuring, fiery serpents were loosed
among the people, biting many of them and causing death. The
people were made conscious of their error and cried to Jehovah
through Moses. Moses made intercession for the people, whereupon God instructed him to make a serpent of brass and set it
upon a standard. When people were bitten they looked upon it
and were healed.

In this act Jesus saw a type of Himself, and in it the Jews should
have seen God's act of benevolence, which would find a fuller and
richer expression of grace unto all. In His conversation with
Nicodemus, Jesus said, "And as Moses lifted up the serpent in the
wilderness, even so must the Son of man be lifted up; that
whosoever believeth may in him have eternal life" (3:14-15). In
the serpents there was the poison of death; in the brazen serpent
there was none, and in their faith to look upon it there was life. So
in Christ there would be none of the poison of sin, but rather the
provision of grace by which they, in their faith, might find the
hope of eternal life. Moses had written of Him.

In the Wilderness of Sin, when Israel had murmured and cried
to the Lord for bread, God gave them the manna from heaven
(Exod. 16). For approximately forty years Jehovah fed them with
this bread; however, although they ate it, they ultimately died. It
could sustain physical life only for a time. But was there no bread
of which a man might eat and live? Jesus saw in this bread a type
of Himself, bread that God gave from heaven for the life of the
world, bread that a man might eat and live (6:33-57). If the Jews
had understood Moses, they should have seen in Him God's
provision for something more than mere physical life; they should
have seen a life like that of the Father—eternal.

The Israelites' thirst for water had been quenched in the wilderness as Moses struck the flinty rock at Rephidim (Exod. 17:1-7; cf.
Deut. 8:15; Ps. 114:8), and at Zin (Num. 20:2-13). Would there
not be some deeper and fuller significance to this than the
quenching of physical thirst? Is there not some deeper thirst of the
human soul than that quenched by water for the body? And
would not God provide for that need? Jesus saw in the providing
of water in the wilderness a type of Himself who would supply the
satisfying drink of life. To the woman of Samaria, He said, "If

thou knewest the gift of God, and who it is that saith to thee, Give me to drink; thou wouldest have asked of him, and he would have given thee living water . . . (and) whosoever drinketh of the water that I shall give him shall never thirst; but the water that I shall give him shall become in him a well of water springing up unto eternal life" (4:10, 14). And again, as He stood before the multitude at the feast of tabernacles, He cried, saying, "He that believeth on me, as the scripture hath said, from within him shall flow rivers of living water" (7:38). In this He was speaking of the Spirit which was yet to be given; in Him would be realized the complete quenching of the thirst of the soul as it pants for God.

The Prophets

As one reads the prophets, he is made conscious of their constant expectation of one to come. Both Jesus and the apostles made repeated appeal to the prophets, for they saw in Jesus the fulfillment of their writings and expectation. All things "must needs be fulfilled which are written in the law of Moses, and the prophets, and the psalms, concerning me," said Jesus. The disciples likewise saw in Him the one of whom Moses and the prophets had written. In their preaching after Pentecost, the apostles made repeated appeal to the testimony and witness of the prophets. As the prophets wrote of the many aspects and characteristics of the Messiah who was to come, they wrote as if they had Him before them in person. In this study only those prophecies recorded by John are considered, for John presented these in the full confidence that their testimony would lead to belief. But it should be remembered that the testimony of the prophets is the testimony of the Father—His testimony through Scripture (5:37-39)—for the prophets spoke His words.

1. His place of birth

In the controversy among the Jews over the question of Jesus' identity, some said, "This is the Christ." However, others questioned this because Jesus was from Galilee, and contended, "Hath not the scripture said that the Christ cometh of the seed of David, and from Bethlehem, the village where David was?" (7:41-42).

The ground of their contention was the testimony of prophecy.

Samuel, whose work marks the actual beginning of the prophetic era, had assured David that of his seed God would raise up one to sit on his throne, that in him God would establish the kingdom, and that the throne would be established for ever (II Sam. 7:12-16). Isaiah had further testified that "unto us a child is born, unto us a son is given . . . Of the increase of his government and of peace there shall be no end, upon the throne of David" (Isa. 9:6-7).

It was Micah who had specified the place of the birth of this one to come when he said, "But thou, Bethlehem Ephrathah, which art little to be among the thousands of Judah, out of thee shall one come forth unto me that is to be ruler in Israel; whose goings forth are from of old, from everlasting" (Mic. 5:2). At this point the Jews were correct; He was to have been born in Bethlehem, the city of David's nativity. Their error was not knowing that Jesus had been born in Bethlehem. Since they were discussing the matter among themselves, and not with Jesus, the matter was not cleared up at the moment. Later this was made clear by other writers (Matthew and Luke); therefore, John passed over it in his Gospel. Jesus, of the seed of David, of the tribe of Judah, born in Bethlehem, fulfilled the expectation of the prophet.

2. The forerunner

When the deputation from Jerusalem asked who he was, John the Baptist declared that he was not the Christ, nor Elijah, nor the prophet. He said simply, "I am the voice of one crying in the wilderness, Make straight the way of the Lord, as said Isaiah the prophet" (1:23). In preparing the people of his day for the Babylonian captivity by comforting them in anticipation of their warfare, the prophet Isaiah had said, "The voice of one that crieth, Prepare ye in the wilderness the way of Jehovah; make level in the desert a highway for our God" (Isa. 40:3). John the Baptist was to open the way for Jesus, to prepare a people for Jesus, and to introduce Him to the Jewish nation. This he did, and in doing it he fulfilled the prophecy of such a one to come.

3. The Spirit

John the Baptist testified that he knew not Jesus as the Messiah, "but he that sent me to baptize in water, he said unto me, Upon whomsoever thou shalt see the Spirit descending, and abiding upon him, the same is he that baptizeth in the Holy Spirit." And further, his testimony was, "I have beheld the Spirit descending as a dove out of heaven; and it abode upon him" (1:32-33).

The coming of the Holy Spirit upon the Messiah had been a matter of prophecy; the manner of His coming had not. Isaiah in particular had given emphasis to the Spirit's abiding upon Him: "And the Spirit of Jehovah shall rest upon him" (Isa. 11:2); "Behold, my servant whom I uphold; my chosen, in whom my soul delighteth: I have put my Spirit upon him" (Isa. 42:1); and, "The Spirit of the Lord Jehovah is upon me" (Isa. 61:1). In speaking of the Redeemer to come, Isaiah had quoted Jehovah further as saying, "my Spirit that is upon thee, and my words which I have put in thy mouth, shall not depart out of thy mouth" (Isa. 59:21). Of this John said concerning Jesus, "For he whom God hath sent speaketh the words of God: for he giveth not the Spirit by measure" (3:34). This was to say that Jesus had received the full measure of the Spirit of God and that the words which He spoke were by that Spirit. To this the prophets had borne witness.

4. The teaching

Jesus came as a teacher. He was recognized by Nicodemus as a teacher come from God. It was by means of teaching that men would be drawn to the Father through Him. When the Jews murmured because of His teaching, His response was, "No man can come to me, except the Father that sent me draw him: and I will raise him up in the last day. It is written in the prophets, And they shall all be taught of God. Every one that hath heard from the Father, and hath learned, cometh unto me" (6:44, 45). Also, through His teaching they should have peace: "These things have I spoken unto you, that in me ye may have peace" (16:33). Of this Isaiah had said, "And all thy children shall be taught of Jehovah; and great shall be the peace of thy children" (Isa. 54:13; 48:16; John 18:20).

Jeremiah had foretold the same thing from a different point of view. Looking at those who should come into covenant relation with God, he had said, "I will put my law in their inward parts, and in their heart will I write it; and I will be their God, and they shall be my people. And they shall teach no more every man his neighbor, and every man his brother, saying, Know Jehovah; for they shall all know me, from the least of them unto the greatest of them, saith Jehovah; for I will forgive their iniquity, and their sin will I remember no more" (Jer. 31:33-34). Jesus fulfilled the word of both Isaiah and Jeremiah; all must be taught of God before they can come into covenant relation with Him. In the days of the Old Covenant, children were born into covenant relation with God and were taught afterward to know Him. Under the New Covenant they shall not be brought into the family of God before being taught. They shall be drawn by teaching, taught first to know Jehovah as His law is impressed on the heart; and then they shall come unto Him. In His teaching at this point, Jesus fulfilled the word of the prophets.

5. The rejected teacher

Because Jesus did not fulfill the preconceived concept of what their Messiah should be, the majority of Jews of Jerusalem rejected Him. As the conflict intensified, it became more and more apparent that the people to whom He had come were not going to receive Him as their Messiah. The teaching only hardened their hearts as they became more and more prejudiced, and the signs made less and less impression on them. John pointed out that this, too, only fulfilled further the words of the prophets: "That the word of Isaiah the prophet might be fulfilled, which he spake, Lord, who hath believed our report? And to whom hath the arm of the Lord been revealed?" (12:38). In his classic poem on the Suffering Servant, Isaiah had foreseen this reaction to the divine effort to save when he said, "Who hath believed our message? and to whom hath the arm of Jehovah been revealed?" (Isa. 53:1). The people had refused to hear Isaiah; likewise they would refuse to hear Him who was to come.

John makes a further appeal to Isaiah in which he shows the moral impossibility of the Jews to believe. In his translation the apostle does not follow either the Hebrew text or the LXX as he says, "For this cause they could not believe, for that Isaiah said again, He hath blinded their eyes, and he hardened their heart; Lest they should see with their eyes, and perceive with their heart, and should turn, and I should heal them. These things said Isaiah, because he saw his glory; and he spake of him" (12:39-41; Isa. 6:9, 10). The impossibility of the Jews responding to Jesus' teaching rests not upon an arbitrary decree of the Father but upon the immutable character of His divine law and the invariable consequence of its violation. Jesus had warned the Jews, "Walk while ye have light, that darkness overtake you not" (12:35). For so long the Jews had refused the light of truth and had so hardened their hearts against it that they were now completely blind. This blindness was the inevitable consequence of living in darkness, making it impossible for them to believe and accept the light of truth. That which Jesus had revealed from the Father was intended to enlighten their minds and soften their hearts, causing them to turn to God. But when they refused to let it accomplish its purpose, God used it to blind, harden, and petrify. The same sun that softens butter hardens putty. The result of softening or hardening depends on the nature of the substance exposed. The Jews had closed their eyes and hardened their hearts, wherefore God completed the blinding and hardening that they could not believe. They and they alone were responsible.

The results which developed in the hearts of the people by Isaiah's preaching were now being completely fulfilled in the people by the word of Him of whom Isaiah wrote. That which Jesus had done in teaching and in the signs given, which were intended to soften the heart and turn the people to God, had only hardened their hearts, making the word imperceptible to their blinded minds.

Zechariah had alluded to this condition of rebellion when he foretold the coming of one who should be king and priest and who should build the temple of Jehovah. According to the prophet, those afar off (the Gentiles) should come and build in this temple erected by the Branch. But concerning those near (the Jews) and their building in the temple, he added, "And this shall come to pass, if ye will diligently obey the voice of Jehovah your God" (Zech. 6:15). They, too, would build if they should obey God's voice. But instead of obeying, they were rejecting the voice of God and therefore would not be permitted to build in the temple which the Branch had come to erect.

6. The King's entrance

Passover was at hand, only six days distant, and the hour had come when He should make Himself known as their King. Earlier, the multitude had offered to crown Him as an earthly king; but this He had rejected (6:15). Now He offers them a spiritual King; and before the week was over, this they rejected.

On the morrow after the sabbath, a large number of Jews who had come to Jerusalem for the feast learned that Jesus was in Bethany and set out to see Him and Lazarus, whom He had raised. Selecting the branches of palm trees, the symbol of festivity and rejoicing (Lev. 23:40), the multitude went out to meet Him. As they came out of the city toward Bethany they cried, "Hosanna (save now): Blessed is he that cometh in the name of the Lord, even the King of Israel" (12:13). Once more the multitude were ready to acclaim Him king. In the excitement of the moment, they thought they were prepared to accept Him as the Messiah. This readiness on their part is indicated by their use of an expression from a definitely messianic psalm, "Blessed be he that cometh in the name of Jehovah" (Ps. 118:26).

Instead of entering the city riding upon a horse, the emblem of worldly power and might, Jesus selected a young ass, the symbol of lowliness (12:14). In this He fulfilled the prediction of Zechariah, who had foretold clearly the method of His entrance into the city and the spirit in which He should come: "Rejoice greatly, O daughter of Zion; shout, O daughter of Jerusalem: behold, thy king cometh unto thee; he is just, and having salvation; lowly, and riding upon an ass, even upon a colt the foal of an ass" (Zech. 9:9). The prophet further emphasizes that the ass was symbolic of the non-political nature of His kingdom, saying, "And I will cut off the chariot from Ephraim, and the horse from Jerusalem; and the battle bow shall be cut off; and he shall speak peace unto the nations: and his dominion shall be from sea to sea, and from the River to the ends of the earth" (Zech. 9:10). The emblems of political grandeur and of military might would have no place in His kingdom.

Later, when the Jews had rejected Him and demanded that He be put to death, Jesus declared to Pilate, "My kingdom (kingship) is not of this world: if my kingdom were of this world, then would my servants fight, that I should not be delivered to the Jews: but now is my kingdom not from hence" (18:36). Three times Pilate sought to save Him, saying, "I find no crime in him" (18:38; 19:4, 6). But because His kingdom was not of this world and because He would not become a king on their terms, the Jews were moved to say, "Away with him, away with him, crucify him! . . . We have no king but Caesar" (19:15). This rejection had been clearly foretold by the prophet who had said, "He was despised, and rejected of men; . . . and as one from whom men hide their face he was despised; and we esteemed him not . . . He was oppressed, yet when he was afflicted he opened not his mouth; as a lamb that is led to the slaughter, and as a sheep that before its shearers is dumb, so he opened not his mouth. By oppression and judgment he was taken away; and as for his generation, who among them considered that he was cut off out of the land of the living for the transgression of my people to whom the stroke was due?" (Isa. 53:3, 7-8).

7. Crucifixion and burial

The mock trial before Pilate was a trial that shall ever be a travesty on the term "justice of the courts." After the governor without evidence had reversed his decision from "innocent" to "guilty," Jesus went out bearing His own cross. The contrast between the tenderness of Him who had loved so fully and warmly and who even now of His own will was laying down His life for others, and the hardness of those who were crucifying Him is demonstrated in their manner of disposing of His garments. Of His regular garments it is said that they divided them; but of the special outer garment, made without seam, they said, "Let us not rend it, but cast lots for it, whose it shall be." In this they fulfilled Scripture: "They part my garments among them, and upon my vesture do they cast lots" (19:24; Ps. 22:18). They were so unimpressed by the scene that they could indifferently spend their time in this way.

Lest the bodies of the three crucified ones should be left on the cross over the Passover, the Jews came to Pilate and requested that the legs be broken that the bodies might be taken away. They broke the legs of the first, but when they came to Jesus they found Him already dead and broke not the legs but pierced His side with a spear (19:31-37). Of this the prophets had written long ago. In his instruction concerning the Passover lamb, Moses had said, "not a bone shall be broken." And the prophet Zechariah had said, "And they shall look unto me whom they have pierced; and they shall mourn for him, as one mourneth for his only son, and shall be in bitterness for him, as one that is in bitterness for his first-born" (Zech. 12:10). Through a prophecy long before uttered, God had pronounced testimony to Jesus' deity.

Joseph of Arimathaea, a rich man, and Nicodemus, who before had come to Him by night, requested the body of Jesus. These two were financially able to provide both spices for the burial and a new tomb in which to place the corpse (19:38-42). Foreseeing this, Isaiah had said, "And they made his grave with the wicked, and with a rich man in his death" (Isa. 53:9). They would have laid Him in the grave with the thieves had not a rich man asked for the body; instead, He was buried in the grave intended for a rich man. This which was done had been foretold long before.

On the morning of the third day, certain disciples came to the tomb to behold, and lo, the stone was rolled away and the tomb was empty. Puzzled, they went away, "For as yet they knew not the scripture, that he must rise again from the dead" (20:9). No special passage is designated. But aside from the psalms, which shall be considered in the next section, Isaiah had said, "When thou shalt make his soul an offering for sin, he shall see his seed, he shall prolong his days, and the pleasure of Jehovah shall prosper in his hand" (Isa. 53:10). By the resurrection His days were prolonged, and in His hand the pleasure of Jehovah has prospered since the momentous event.

Jesus was the theme of prophecy; and these prophecies all testify that He is the Son of God, the seed of David, the bright and morning star, the hope of the world. Prophecy, fulfilled in Him, stands as a monument to the fact that God has spoken and that Jesus is the Christ, the Son of God.

The Psalms

Seven times in John's Gospel appeal is made to the psalms. All except one are psalms of David; the other is a psalm of Asaph, which Jesus used in making a charge against the people, saying, "Is it not written in your law, I said, Ye are gods?" (10:34; Ps. 82:6). The psalm from which He quoted bears the title "Unjust Judgments Rebuked," and in it unjust judges and judgments were rebuked by Jehovah. The Jews had unjustly judged Jesus, accusing Him of blasphemy. From the law to which they appealed He convicted them of the same guilt as that of the judges in the days of Asaph.

Is there significance in the fact that the psalms appealed to are psalms of David? The indication is that there is. The prophets had foretold the coming of a "David," who should be the king of the kingdom of God. Hosea was the earliest to designate the king to come as David, when he said, "Afterward shall the children of Israel return, and seek Jehovah their God, and David their king, and shall come with fear unto Jehovah and to his goodness in the latter days" (Hos. 3:5). "Afterward" designates relation to the captivity: "David their king" identifies the king as the seed of David prophesied by Samuel (II Sam. 7:11-14); "with fear" expresses the reverence and respect for the Lord with which they shall come; and "in the latter days" reveals the time, for the expression is always used of the messianic era.

About one hundred years after Hosea, Jeremiah quotes Jehovah as saying, "behold, the days come, saith Jehovah, that I will raise unto David a righteous Branch, and he shall reign as king and deal wisely, and shall execute justice and righteousness in the land" (Jer. 23:5). This "righteous Branch" of David is identified by the prophet as "David," "but they shall serve Jehovah their God, and David their king, whom I will raise up unto them" (Jer. 30:9). The character of His reign as one of wise dealings and execution of justice and righteousness identifies the reign as identical with the character of Jehovah's reign (Ps. 89:14; 97:2-3).

Ezekiel, contemporary with Jeremiah but serving in Babylon, likewise spoke of "David," whom Jehovah would raise up: "And I will set up one shepherd over them, and he shall feed them, even my servant David; he shall feed them, and he shall be their shepherd. And I, Jehovah, will be their God, and my servant David prince among them" (Ezek. 34:23, 24). "And my servant David shall be king over them; and they all shall have one shepherd; they shall also walk in mine ordinances, and observe my statutes, and do them" (Ezek. 37:24). Ezekiel emphasizes the shepherding and feeding aspect of the reign of this David.

As the new David, descendant of David of old, the Messiah would share in the experiences of the former David. David of old had realized the failure of his immediate house to fulfill Jehovah's promises to him, so he had looked to the coming of one after him who would fulfill the hope of his own heart and who would in some way share his own experiences. In his "last words" the king had said, "The God of Israel said, the Rock of Israel spake to me:

One that ruleth over men righteously, That ruleth in the fear of God, He shall be as the light of the morning, when the sun riseth, A morning without clouds, When the tender grass springeth out of the earth, Through clear shining after rain." In this statement the psalmist saw the freshness and beauty of the reign of the ruler. But as if in a tone of sadness and regret, followed by a feeling of certainty, he continued, "Verily my house is not so with God; Yet he hath made with me an everlasting covenant, Ordered in all things, and sure: For it is all my salvation, and all my desire, Although he maketh it not to grow." The prophet followed this with a second description of the one to come, describing the iron hand with which he must deal with his enemies: "But the ungodly shall be all of them as thorns to be thrust away, Because they cannot be taken with the hand; But the man that toucheth them Must be armed with iron and the staff of a spear: And they shall be utterly burned with fire in their place" (II Sam. 23:3-7). Fresh and tender toward His own, but strong and just with His enemies, would be the David of promise.

In this expectation the ancient prophet and king spoke often in his psalms of the one to come. In some of them, he spoke directly of the king to come; in others he saw him sharing some of his own experiences, finding fulfillment in a larger and fuller manner than his own.

1. Zeal (Ps. 69:9)

David was in sore distress because of his enemies. His cry was, "Because for thy sake I have borne reproach; Shame hath covered my face." Because of his relation to the Lord, he had become a stranger to his brethren and an alien to his mother's children. His summary of the cause for this condition was, "For the zeal of thy house hath eaten me up; And the reproaches of them that reproach thee are fallen upon me" (Ps. 69:7-9).

In the city of Jerusalem, Jesus had driven both sheep and oxen out of the temple and had poured out the changers' money. And to them that sold the doves He had said, "Take these things hence; make not my Father's house a house of merchandise" (2:13-16). The disciples saw in this the fulfillment of the word of David, for they "remembered that it was written, Zeal for thy house shall eat me up" (v. 17). By this act, manifesting the zeal of His illustrious ancestor, Jesus was alienating from Himself the Jews of Jerusalem and His own brethren as well. David's word was finding its fulfillment in Him who came.

2. Familiar friend (Ps. 41:9)

As He addressed the disciples while He ate the last supper with them, Jesus urged them to follow the example He had given in the washing of their feet. He assured them that the blessing of knowing was in doing the things they knew should be done. He then said, "I speak not of you all: I know whom I have chosen: but that the scripture may be fulfilled, He that eateth my bread lifted up his heel against me" (13:18). Possible allusion to this same Scripture was made when He said in His prayer to the Father, "I guarded them, and not one of them perished, but the son of perdition; that the scripture might be fulfilled" (17:12).

In a time of sickness, the psalmist had cried unto God of his enemies who spoke evil of him and who went about speaking falsehood against him. The sorest trial of all seemed to be summed up when he said, "Yea, mine own familiar friend, in whom I trusted, Who did eat of my bread, Hath lifted up his heel against me" (Ps. 41:9). This same experience of deceit and betrayal was now being experienced by the second David as Judas betrayed Him into the hands of His enemies.

The perfidy of Judas is more fully realized when one understands the significance which the people of the East attach to the eating of bread with another. It was betrayal of the worst sort to break a covenant made through eating together.[1] This had been the experience of David which was now shared in a fuller measure by the second David, who was betrayed by Judas, with whom He had eaten so often.

3. Hated without a cause (Pss. 35:19; 69:4)

David had prayed, "Let not them that are mine enemies wrongfully rejoice over me; Neither let them wink with the eye that hate me without a cause" (Ps. 35:19). And in a cry of distress, he had

---

1. Baker's *Dictionary of Theology,* "Eating," pp. 175, 176.

lamented, "They that hate me without a cause are more than the hairs of my head" (Ps. 69:4).

This experience likewise found expression in the life of Jesus. It appears that such an attitude of the wicked toward the righteous is the experience of them that would do right. Rejected by the Jews, among whom He had done His mighty works which were witness of the Father to His Sonship, He charged that the Jews hated both Him and His Father. "But this cometh to pass," He said, "that the word may be fulfilled that is written in their law, They hated me without a cause" (15:24, 25). His enemies wrongfully hated Him. As in the case of the first David, they hated Him without a cause; they could prove no sin in Him. They could convict Him of no sin, and this only intensified the hatred.

4. Crucifixion: parting His garments (Ps. 22:18; John 19:24)

Their hatred without a cause led the Jews to demand the death of Jesus by crucifixion. Probably no psalm more graphically describes the scene of the crucifixion than the twenty-second, a psalm of David. The psalm begins with a cry of one forsaken, "My God, My God, why hast thou forsaken me?" (v. 1). It continues with a description of others who, in their crying to God, had been heard and delivered; but this one is lowly and despised of the people (vv. 4-6). A mocking crowd is described as laughing to scorn the sufferer and as shooting out the lip, shaking the head, and saying, Let Jehovah deliver and rescue him. There follows a description of one surrounded by strong bulls of Bashan who have beset him; they open wide the mouth at him, as a roaring lion they seek his destruction. He is poured out like water; his heart is like wax; his strength is dried up; his tongue cleaves to the jaws as he is brought into the dust of death. A company of evil-doers close in upon him; they pierce his hands and his feet; yet he may count all his bones. They look; they stare; "they part my garments among them, And upon my vesture do they cast lots" (v. 18). Then there is a cry to Jehovah to be not far off but to deliver the soul from the sword and his life from the power of the dog, from the lion's mouth, and from the wild-ox (vv. 19-21).

Surely the psalmist was not speaking of himself except in a figurative way as his enemies sought his own life. But in the Spirit of prophecy, he looked to his descendant, the illustrious David of the future, who should come. He saw the utter loneliness of one forsaken of God for a small moment, sharing the experience of the sinner in his eternal separation from God, crying to the Father. He saw in vision what John saw in fact: the son of David was mocked and crucified, bearing alone the reproaches of the lost which were being heaped upon Him. John beheld the soldiers who had crucified Jesus as they took His garments, dividing them into four parts among themselves until they came to the coat or tunic which was woven in one piece from top to bottom. This they would not rend, but rather said, "Let us . . . cast lots for it, whose it shall be," to which John adds, "that the scripture might be fulfilled, which saith, They parted my garments among them, And upon my vesture did they cast lots" (19:24). The vision of the first David was now fulfilled in the second David.

5. Gall and vinegar (Ps. 69:21; John 19:28-30)

In the same psalm of distress in which David had lamented, "They that hate me without a cause are more than the hairs of my head" (Ps. 69:4), and, "For the zeal of thy house hath eaten me up" (v. 9), the prophet also made the complaint, "They gave me also gall for my food; and in my thirst they gave me vinegar to drink" (v. 21).

This experience of the psalmist of the bitter treatment heaped upon him, whether figurative or a literal incident in his life, now found fulfillment in Him who came after. Jesus had been nailed to the cross, the soldiers had parted His garments and cast lots for the tunic, and He had made provision for the care of His mother. John describes the scene that followed, saying, "After this Jesus, knowing that all things are now finished, that the scripture might be accomplished, saith, I thirst. There was set there a vessel full of vinegar: so they put a sponge full of the vinegar upon hyssop, and brought it to his mouth. When Jesus therefore had received the vinegar, he said, It is finished: and he bowed his head, and gave up his spirit" (19:28-30). Here we see the human Jesus suffering and thirsting; but in His fulfilling the word of God, we see the testimony of His Father that He is the Christ, the Son of God.

6. The resurrection (Pss. 22:22-31; 16:10)

John makes no direct reference to the psalms in recording the resurrection of Jesus. Jesus had indicated His resurrection when

He said, "Destroy this temple, and in three days I will raise it up . . . But he spake of the temple of his body" (2:19, 21). John adds, "When therefore he was raised from the dead, his disciples remembered that he spake this; and they believed the scripture, and the word which Jesus had said" (v. 22). It has been pointed out that Isaiah had foretold the resurrection and that Jesus had fulfilled the prediction.

But what, if anything, had the psalmists said about His being raised? No particular psalm is quoted by John, and he truly says, "For as yet they knew not the scripture, that he must rise again from the dead" (20:9). However, the resurrection fulfilled the hope expressed in several of the psalms. Two are here considered.

In Psalm 22, in which the crucifixion was foretold, the latter part seems clearly to point to the activities following the untimely end of the one put to death. "I will declare thy name unto my brethren: In the midst of the assembly will I praise thee" (v. 22). His cry had been heard (v. 24); and the praise offered is "in the great assembly" (v. 25). The "great assembly" would include the Gentiles, "all the kindreds of the nations shall worship before thee" (v. 27). The kingdom would be Jehovah's; "a seed shall serve him, It shall be told of the Lord unto the next generation"; and His righteousness shall be declared "unto a people that shall be born, that he hath done it" (vv. 30-31). These things which should follow the death described in verses 1-21 clearly indicate that death did not end the experience of the sufferer but that it was through the triumph of death that He should accomplish the deliverance and praise of men of all the earth. It is a prophet's description of the triumph of Jesus, and the Father's testimony to Him that He is His Son.

The clearest prophecy of the resurrection found in the psalms is in Psalm 16. Here again David speaks not of himself but of one in whom this hope should be realized: "For thou wilt not leave my soul to Sheol; Neither wilt thou suffer thy holy one to see (i.e., experience) corruption" (v. 10). David's tomb continued with the Jews; he himself knew that he spoke not of himself, but of another, for he said, "I am going the way of all the earth" (I Kings 2:2). David's prophecy was the cry of the human heart for life beyond this and the expression of hope of its realization in the promised seed.

Summary

Jesus fulfilled all things written of Him in the writings of Moses, the prophets, and the psalms. In these is God's witness to the deity of Jesus, to the fact that He is the Christ, the Son of the living God. This is testimony that one can see and hear and examine for himself. The conclusion of the syllogism at the beginning of the chapter can be none other than that Jesus is the Christ, and the word is the word of God. For,

1. Man of himself cannot foretell events of history or the coming and actions of an individual. Only a supernatural power can do this.

2. The Bible foretold events to come and of a person whom God should raise up, which events were fulfilled in due time.

3. Therefore, the Bible is not of man, but supernatural in its origin and teaching, and bears irrefutable evidence to the deity of Jesus Christ.

The Father's Testimony —The Empty Tomb

8

John's final testimony of the Father to the deity of Jesus is the testimony of the empty tomb—the resurrection of Jesus. Many excellent treatises have been written on this theme. The factuality of the event has been made from every point of view imaginable, including theological, philosophical, psychological, and scientific approaches. In this chapter only the fact of the empty tomb and the evidence for the resurrection as presented by John will be considered. An additional word on some of the contrary theories which have been advanced will be given.

Early in His ministry Jesus declared the anticipated resurrection of His body when He said, "Destroy this temple, and in three days I will raise it up ... But he spake of the temple of his body" (2:19, 21). It is folly for one to argue any resurrection other than that of the body of Jesus, for this is the only resurrection known to Scripture. When Jesus spoke of "the temple," John understood Him to mean "the temple of his body." The empty tomb indicated that what had been put in the sepulcher was gone. The body, not His spirit or His cause, had been wrapped in grave cloths; but that which had been so wrapped had somehow left the tomb. The bodily resurrection is the only resurrection that will satisfy the facts of Scripture.

Belief in the resurrection rests upon testimony. Either the testimony is sufficiently strong to convince, or it is not. If it is of such weight, belief results; if not, then one cannot be held responsible for not believing that Jesus was raised. However, to refute the evidence one must find a flaw in the testimony, prove an ulterior motive for fraud, or produce fresh evidence that would discredit the evidence offered. If this cannot be done, then the evidence stands and one must believe that Jesus is the Christ. The question is whether the evidence for the resurrection as presented by John is sufficiently clear and strong to produce faith. Millions who have weighed it fairly, desiring to know the way to God, have found it sufficient. But each must weigh it and decide for himself.

The Empty Tomb

According to John, after Jesus died upon the cross, Joseph of Arimathaea and Nicodemus came to Pilate and asked that they be given the body for burial. The body was laid in a new tomb near the site of the crucifixion. John passes over many of the details recorded by the other writers, especially such details as the sealing of the tomb, the request of the Pharisees for a guard, the placing of the guard, the report of the guard, and the giving of money to the soldiers to keep silent. John comes directly to the evidence of the empty tomb.

1. The open sepulcher—the stone removed

John testifies that on the first day of the week while it was yet early, Mary Magdalene came to the place of burial, "and seeth the stone taken away from the tomb" (20:1). This raises questions which, though trite, must nevertheless be answered before any reasonable conclusion can be given for the removal other than that it was by divine act. If it was removed, who removed it? Were they from among the Romans, the Jews, or the disciples? Since the friends of Jesus were intimidated by both the Jews and the Romans, it seems utterly unlikely that they would have the courage to attempt such an undertaking. Also, with the tomb guarded by Roman soldiers, they would face the seemingly impossible task of removing the stone and then the body. All reasonable conclusions would eliminate the friends of Jesus as the ones involved in removing the stone. If it be argued that the enemies of Jesus had removed the stone, then question arises as to which of them would have done it. The Jews would not, for they were the ones who sought the security of a guard. The Romans would not, for failure on their part to carry out an assignment meant death. Actually, there is no evidence, old or new, to indicate that either group was responsible.

A second question would ask why the stone was removed. Was it removed by a group who wished to steal the body? Was it removed to allow the body of Jesus to leave? Or was it to allow the disciples to look in and to enter? If we say it was opened in order to steal the body, we are faced with the question of which group attempted to steal it and how they accomplished the task. Second, if God had raised the body, it does not seem necessary for the tomb to have been opened in order that the body might leave. It had undergone changes during the time it lay in the tomb, as indicated by the sudden appearance of Jesus within the midst of the disciples upon two occasions in which the door was barred (20:19, 26). The probability appears to be the third; the stone was removed so that the disciples might enter and see for themselves that the body was gone. This is what took place (vv. 5, 6).

2. The body gone—the empty tomb

When Mary came to the tomb and found the stone rolled away, she found also that the body was not in the sepulcher. The same questions raised regarding the removal of the stone are now raised concerning the body which was gone. Were those who removed the body friends or enemies? If they were friends, which ones were they? Why would they remove it and how would they have removed it? The evidence is clear that Mary did not know it had been removed (v. 2); nor did Peter and the disciple who was with him know of such removal. They testify that the body was gone, but at first they had no explanation for what had happened.

3. The grave clothes

Apparently John was the first disciple to arrive at the tomb. He was content to pause at the opening, stoop, and look in. But upon the arrival of Peter, both entered. They saw the linen cloths lying, "and the napkin, that was upon his head, not lying with the linen cloths, but rolled up in a place by itself" (vv. 6-7). We learn from the description of Lazarus as he emerged from the tomb that the napkin was placed about the face separate from the rest of the clothes (11:44).

The description of the linen cloths and the napkin indicates that there had been no hurry to get away and that the body had not been stolen. If the body had been stolen, no one would have spent time removing the cloths and the napkin. These testify that Jesus came out of them as easily as He entered the room through closed doors; they testify that a change had taken place in the body.

This evidence was convincing to John. Of himself he said, "and he saw, and believed. For as yet they (he and Peter) knew not the scripture, that he must rise again from the dead" (vv. 8, 9). The apostle now believed that Jesus had been raised from the dead and that Scripture, which hitherto had held little meaning to him, was beginning to be understood. The open tomb, the absent body, and the orderly arrangement of the napkin and grave cloths were convincing evidence of the resurrection.

The Appearances of Jesus

John records four appearances of Jesus to various disciples. Two of the appearances were on the day of His disappearance from the tomb, the third was a week later, and the fourth sometime following.

1. To Mary Magdalene

Mary had come early to the tomb on the first day after the sabbath. She was first to discover that the stone had been rolled away, and she reported it to Peter and John. She returned to the tomb and, looking in, beheld two angels where the body had lain, one at the head and the other at the foot. She was looking for the body of Jesus and asked them where it might have been taken. She turned and saw Jesus but did not recognize Him. He asked her two simple questions, "Why weepest thou? whom seekest thou?" (20:15). The question, "Whom seekest thou?" should have focused the attention on a person rather than an object, the corpse

(Hendriksen). Jesus' one word, "Mary," opened her eyes to see that it was Jesus. Her response was one of recognition, "Rabboni!" which is in the Hebrew, "Teacher."

Jesus was now different; not only had the body undergone change, as indicated by His leaving the grave clothes, but also there was a difference in His relation to Mary. This latter is indicated in His reply, "Touch me not; for I am not yet ascended unto the Father." It was not a point of touching Jesus, for later Jesus urged Thomas to touch both His hand and His side; but other matters were involved. By the charge, "Touch me not," Jesus assured Mary that the old relation was now changed; she was not to keep clinging to Him as though the "little while" of which He had spoken was now past. Also, Mary must learn that He for whom she longed was not to be hers forever as her Lord and King or as an abiding companion until He had ascended to the Father. Therefore, "Go unto my brethren," a closer and more endearing relation than "friends" or "servants," "and say to them, I ascend unto my Father and your Father, and my God and your God" (v. 17). He was now ready to ascend to the Father from whence He had come. His use of "my Father and your Father" and "my God and your God" marks a clear concept in Jesus' mind of the difference between Himself and His brethren, although He had shared a common humanity with them.

2. To the disciples

His second appearance was made to the disciples on the evening of that day, the first day, when Jesus appeared to them in a room to which the doors were shut. The word *shut* is from *kleiō*, "shut, lock, bar" (Arndt and Gingrich). The usual use of the word in the New Testament indicates the idea of something shut and unable to be opened, hence locked or barred (see Matt. 25:10; Luke 11:7; Acts 21:30; Rev. 3:7, 8; 20:3; 21:25). The account indicates a sudden appearance of Jesus in the room, though He did not enter through one of the doors.

The first words of Jesus to the disciples were, "Peace be unto you" (v. 19). He then showed them His hands and His side, that they might be assured that the one in their midst was the Jesus whom they had known. The effect of this was joy: they "were glad, when they saw the Lord" (v. 20). On the ground of their

acceptance of Him, He would now send them forth as the Father
had sent Him. The Father had sent Him to speak His words and to
do His will, so now Jesus would send these to speak His words and
to do His will. Their power to forgive or retain sins would be
strictly as He should give them instructions from Himself.

3. To Thomas and the eleven

Thomas was absent from the eleven at the time Jesus appeared
unto them. When the disciples saw Thomas, their testimony was,
"We have seen the Lord," but he was skeptical. His response was,
"Except I shall see in his hands the print of the nails, and put my
finger into the print of the nails, and put my hand into his side, I
will not believe" (v. 25). He was demanding the evidence of sight
and touch. One week later the skepticism of Thomas was ex-
ploded. As before, Jesus appeared in their midst with "the doors
being shut." This time Thomas was present. Jesus said to him,
"Reach hither thy finger, and see my hands; and reach hither thy
hand, and put it into my side: and be not faithless, but believing"
(v. 27). The evidence was conclusive; Thomas' reply was one of
deep conviction and assurance as he responded, "My Lord and my
God" (v. 28). No greater assurance of one's conviction could ever
have been elicited than the reply of Thomas. It would have been
the height of blasphemy for a Jew to have recognized any man
with the words of Thomas; but when one hears them spoken of
Jesus, one feels that Thomas spoke not blasphemy but rather that
he spoke the truth.

4. To the disciples by Galilee

After some days (John does not specify the number), Jesus
appeared to the disciples by the sea of Tiberias. Seven of them had
decided to go fishing; they had toiled all night but had taken
nothing. As day was breaking they saw the form of a man on the
beach but knew not who it was. After asking them if they had
caught anything, to which they replied, "No," the one on the
shore told them to cast the net on the right side of the boat. They
followed His instructions and the net was filled. John then recognized the figure of Jesus. Peter, following his usual impulsive
nature, plunged into the water and swam to shore. This was the
third appearance of Jesus to the disciples.

After the disciples had eaten their breakfast, Jesus began to press Peter for an answer to the question, "lovest thou me more than these?" (21:15). Whether Jesus intended the phrase "more than these" to indicate the other disciples, thus asking if Peter loved Him more than did these disciples, or whether He intended the question to include such items as the nets, boat, and occupation of fishing, is left indefinite. Inasmuch as John does not include in his Gospel the boast of Peter, "If all shall be offended in thee, I will never be offended" (Matt. 26:33), it is possible that the question to Peter referred only to the fishing equipment. In either case it is clear that Jesus intended to bring to Peter's mind the threefold denial by insisting upon a threefold confession of his love.

As Peter continued to hedge, trying to avoid a direct answer, the Lord continued to ask and to instruct him to "feed my lambs," "tend my sheep," "feed my sheep," and "follow me." Peter accepted this trust; and he remained true to it, thereby proving his conviction that Jesus was the Messiah who had been raised from the dead.

The Effect upon Those to Whom Jesus Appeared

1. Mary

From Mary Magdalene, a frustrated and grieved disciple, came the first herald of the good news of the resurrection. Immediately after seeing Jesus she came to the disciples with the testimony, "I have seen the Lord; and that he had said these things unto her" (20:18). The things He had said to her were, "Touch me not; for I am not yet ascended unto the Father: but go unto my brethren, and say to them, I ascend unto my Father and your Father, and my God and your God" (v. 17). There was no question in her mind; Jesus had been raised from the dead.

2. Peter

What was the effect of Mary's testimony upon Peter? The apostle lost no time in hurrying with the other disciple to the tomb; in his excitement he ran to it. One cannot help wondering if

Peter's conscience was not pricking him as he remembered the three times he denied even an acquaintance with the Lord at a time when Jesus needed him most. This is possible, but, of course, not certain. True to his impetuous nature, Peter did not hesitate to enter immediately into the tomb. The impression of the empty tomb was so profound that from the day of Pentecost until the end of his life Peter remained a faithful and loyal witness to this central event in history—the resurrection of Jesus from the dead. Upon and around this great fact he built all his preaching.

3. John

Throughout his Gospel, John manifests the characteristics of a keen observer of details. He never overlooks the smallest details. He never overlooks the smallest events, numbers, and proximity of items which go to make a dependable witness. It is John who tells us of the linen cloths lying in one place and of the napkin in another. It is he who tells us that when the side of Jesus was pierced, "there came out blood and water" (19:34). It is he who related the number of fishes, one hundred and fifty-three, taken on that memorable morning after they had worked all night and caught nothing. It is also he who was first to grasp the significance of the removed stone, the empty tomb, and the location of the linen cloths and the folded napkin. Having entered the tomb, "he saw, and believed" (20:8). By inference one supposes that Peter, his companion, did not at the time grasp the full significance of what he saw.

Throughout the rest of his life, John was a witness to the things which he had seen. Of the water and blood that flowed from the side of the crucified one, John says, "And he that hath seen hath borne witness, and his witness is true: and he knoweth that he saith true, that ye also may believe" (19:35). The Gospel which he wrote is his testimony to the fact of the empty tomb and its evidence that Jesus is the Christ, the Son of God. Until it is shown that John's testimony contains some ulterior motive or inconsistencies and flaws that would nullify it, or until fresh evidence is produced to offset it, his witness will remain such as would stand in any court of law. It is the witness of one whose character has not been impeached and who was competent both physically and mentally to testify.

4. The disciples

For fear of the Jews, the disciples had met together behind "shut doors," both on the day of the resurrection and again eight days later (20:19, 26). From this fearful mood and disposition they were transformed into bold and courageous men—men who changed the thinking of the world by their preaching. They themselves explained this change as having been wrought by the empty tomb—by the resurrection of Jesus from the dead (e.g., I Pet. 1:3-5; I John 3:1-3; etc.).

Their change in attitude is explained only on the ground of the resurrection of Jesus. The change and its impact upon the world become in turn witnesses to the resurrection. Beginning in Jerusalem, without money and without social or political prestige, this handful of disciples was able to do what the Roman Empire with all its military and political power was unable to do. It was able to conquer the world and bring into existence a kingdom under one King, a kingdom that was to pass through manifold trials and testings but destined to stand forever. Truly their achievement is a monument to the resurrection of Jesus from the dead.

5. Thomas

The change wrought in Thomas by the empty tomb is probably the most remarkable of them all. From the skeptic who said, "Except I shall see in his hands the print of the nails, and put my finger into the print of the nails, and put my hand into his side, I will not believe" (20:25), he was led to exclaim, "My Lord and my God" (20:28). For a Jew to say such was either blasphemy of the highest sort or the expression of a firm conviction, based on evidence, that must be declared at any price.

In relating this confession of Thomas, John appears to reach the climax of evidence and its effect on men. The pessimist (11:16) and skeptic among the group was brought to acknowledge Jesus as Lord and God. There could have been no greater confession of faith or of conviction that Christ had been raised from the dead than the expression of Thomas.

Alternatives to the Resurrection

In relating the account of the closing events of Jesus' life, John presents four facts: (1) Jesus actually died on the cross; (2) His body was taken down from the cross and buried in a tomb; (3) on the morning of the third day, He arose from the dead; and (4) afterward He appeared to Mary, to the disciples upon two occasions, and to seven others by the Sea of Galilee. These are related as facts and were believed by the early Christians.

Many hypotheses have been advanced through the centuries that have attempted to explain the mystery of the triumph of the cause of Christ without accepting the fact of the resurrection of Jesus. No one has questioned the fact that the early Christians, and Christians from that day till now, have believed that Christ was raised from the dead. The problem that has faced skeptics, and faces them today, is that of accounting for this belief in the resurrection. The genesis of the movement and its history that followed demand an explanation. Some explanations that have been offered through the years are briefly presented.

1. The swoon hypothesis

The swoon hypothesis holds that Jesus did not actually die, but that due to the pain and torture of the cross He swooned upon it. It was thought by both friends and foes that He had died, but both were in error at this point. They buried Him in the tomb, where He revived, removed the stone, and appeared to the disciples. Overjoyed at the appearance, they began to preach that He had been raised from the dead.

This assumption evades, avoids, and overlooks the facts associated with the event. First, it does not take into consideration the physical condition of Jesus at the time of the crucifixion. The week prior to the event had been a full and tense one. Jesus had had no rest the night before the crucifixion. He had spent the earlier part of it with the disciples, the middle part in praying, and the latter part in the mock trials through which He was dragged. This was followed by scourging and finally by the crucifixion itself. Physically, He would have been exhausted.

Second, the supposition avoids the fact that Jesus was crucified by His enemies, men who would be sure that He was dead. The Roman soldiers were no novices in this work. When they came to His body, they were so certain that He was dead that they did not break His legs, but instead, pierced His side, from which came water and blood. The hole left by the spear was large enough that

Jesus told Thomas to reach forth his fist and put it into the wound left by the spear. Further, one wonders from where came food and water and medical care for one in such condition, who for three days was entombed in complete isolation. In His weakened and wounded condition these would be essential.

Third, the nail-torn hands and feet are overlooked by those who defend the swoon hypothesis, contending that He removed the stone from the mouth of the tomb. These stones were heavy and were rolled into the mouth of the hewn tomb in such a way that it would be virtually impossible to remove them from within, especially with hands swollen and bloody from the recent piercing of the nails. Also there was the loss of blood from the hands and feet, as well as that which had flowed from the pierced side, leaving Him feeble and weak. Was it possible for one who was in this weakened condition and so near death that both friends and foes thought Him dead to revive sufficiently to remove the stone?

Fourth, had He succeeded in all this, how was He to escape the Roman soldiers set to guard the tomb? Are we asked to believe that all these were so lax in attending their job that they neither heard nor saw what was taking place? Are we required to believe further that if all these things had been the explanation, both Jesus and the disciples would have been so dishonest as to have knowingly deceived the world with their story of the resurrection? Further, would the world have been so naive as to have accepted their falsehood? Reason has a tendency to revolt against such unfounded deductions.

Fifth, what happened to Jesus after He revived from the swoon? It seems an incredulous supposition that He could have kept Himself secret from the world until He died a natural death and that the disciples could then give to Him a normal burial without the deceit being detected. The hypothesis is too implausible to satisfy the facts. It appears that those who subscribe to this theory are inconsistent in charging gullibility to Christians.

2. The theft of the body

This hypothesis takes a turn in two directions: one, that the disciples stole the body, and the second, that the enemies of Jesus stole the body. The latter may be dismissed on the ground that the enemies could have no motive for stealing the body, inasmuch as it was they who demanded the guard to prohibit the body from being stolen.

The theft of the body by the disciples may be dismissed on the ground of two impossibilities, one physical, the other moral. First, it would have been physically impossible for the disciples to have stolen the body because of the Roman guard. To charge the Roman guard with having allowed any group to steal the body is to express ignorance of the discipline of Roman soldiers and of the consequences for such laxity of duty. The conjecture that the body was stolen from the tomb poses a physical impossibility.

Second, had the first difficulty, by some extraordinary happening, been overcome, a greater difficulty is confronted in the moral impossibility of such an action. In the light of all the evidence extant, Jesus had taught the highest code of morals known to man. Beginning on Pentecost the disciples followed the steps of the Master in teaching the same high standard of morality. They condemned lying, deceit, and hypocrisy. For them to have built such a system of ethics and morals on a foundation of lies and deception is from a moral point of view highly improbable if not impossible.

Third, these men who founded the church on the fact of the resurrection gave their lives as testimony to their conviction of Jesus' deity, which they based on the resurrection. Men deceive, lie, and act falsely only as there are motives for such actions. No adequate motive has ever been discovered for their lying in this matter. They gained neither wealth nor prestige by their testimony and teaching. On the contrary, they were driven from place to place and were despised and rejected of men; many of them met a martyr's death because of their testimony. In the face of facts, the theft of the body by friends or foes is virtually impossible to accept.

3. The vision hypothesis

The hypothesis most widely held a few decades ago, and still held by many even today, is the vision hypothesis. This assumption affords little comfort, as it only substitutes one miracle for another. Subscribers to this supposition hold that Jesus was not raised from the dead but that the body remained in the tomb and that He appeared to the disciples in a vision. In this vision He appeared to them in a glorified state.

Three objections may be registered against this improbable theory. First, as suggested above, it substitutes one miracle for another. If one can accept the miracle of a vision, why not accept the miracle of the resurrection of the body? Second, the hypothesis does not do justice to the empty tomb. The body was gone, and this must be accounted for. Third, it does not do justice to the gospel story. From the beginning the disciples preached the bodily resurrection of Jesus from the dead and built the entire hope of Christianity on this fact. It makes false the claims of the apostles that their eyes beheld Him, their hands handled Him, and their ears heard Him after He was raised. The conjecture would have to defend the possibility of a spiritual kingdom of truth having error and falsehood for its foundation.

4. Various other hypotheses

There are various other hypotheses that have been advanced through the years: (a) The so-called "cause" theory, which says that it was the "cause" or spirit of Jesus that was raised as the cause for which He died was revived in the disciples. The answer to this is simple. It was not the cause but the body of Jesus that was placed in the tomb. (b) The optical illusion hypothesis suggests that all they saw was what we would call a "ghost." They were so overwrought that what they saw was not a spirit, but someone whom they thought was Jesus. (c) The hallucination hypothesis claims that the illusion was in their own minds. They were in such a state of shock that for the moment they were deranged.

God's answer to every one of these hypotheses has been the empty tomb. After one has explored these hypotheses and has done his best to build under them some kind of foundation that will satisfy the peculiar type of mind that these would appeal to, he is yet faced with the fact that *the tomb was empty.* He must explain what happened to the body, how it happened, and how the body was removed in the face of the pains taken by the Jews and Romans to see that nothing should happen to it. Through the centuries the empty tomb has been the Gibraltar of Christian faith and the Waterloo of skeptics.

5. The "joke" hypothesis

It has seemed to this writer that if one were looking for a purely speculative hypothesis which accounts for the empty tomb, without admitting the resurrection of Jesus, the most plausible view of them all has been overlooked. This suggestion has never been seen in print or heard of by the writer; it is one that occurred to him as being better than any or all he has read.

Why not suggest the hypothesis that since Pilate's utter disgust with the Jews was known by Roman soldiers, they came to Pilate and suggested that they play a prank on the Jews. It would be terribly humiliating to the Jews should the body disappear. And so they ventured to present the idea to the Roman pontiff. The governor was so delighted with the possibility of humiliating the Jewish rulers that he allowed the soldiers themselves to remove the body and then suggest that it had been raised from the dead. This would thoroughly embarrass the Jews. This gave the followers of Jesus the very thing they needed, evidence that the body had been raised. So that is how it all began. This at least explains the empty tomb.

Of course, the fault with this assumption is that it is nearly two thousand years too late and has not one iota of evidence to sustain it. It is contrary to all the facts and hardly takes into consideration that Pilate was in no humor at the time for a joke of any kind. So, like all the other so-called theories, the joke would be on the one who should subscribe to it. The only logical answer to the empty tomb is that God raised Jesus from the dead and that the resurrection is God's conclusive witness to the fact that Jesus is the Christ, His only begotten Son.

The Testimony of Jesus — His Moral Glory 9

That which is here designated "Christ's Moral Glory" consists of the perfections which marked His earthly life and ministry. These perfections are manifested in the harmony of His life and conduct with His teaching. There must be the proper integration of the ideas as presented in one's teaching with the teacher's conduct in relation to the teaching if the words of a teacher are to be deemed worthy of acceptance. In this ideal relation of life and teaching is found further evidence to the deity of Jesus.

The proposition of the chapter is this: the teaching of Jesus and His relation to that teaching, as revealed in the Gospel of John, are such that they can be only the product of divine origin. The issue may be stated in the words of the multitude in Jerusalem: "And many of them said, He hath a demon, and is mad; why hear ye him?" Others said, "These are not the sayings of one possessed with a demon. Can a demon open the eyes of the blind?" (10:20-21). This draws the issue clearly: either (1) He is mad and possessed of a demon, or (2) He is the Christ, as proved by His sayings and deeds. But the sayings and deeds are of such nature and are so perfectly integrated that they completely refute the demon and madman charge. This leaves the one alternative: He is of God.

Jesus had made the challenge, "If any man willeth to do his (God's) will, he shall know of the teaching, whether it is of God, or whether I speak from myself" (7:17). The challenge to His hearers to investigate His teaching implies that when one investigates he will be convinced that the substance of Jesus' teaching is not that of a man, but of God. The nature of the teaching, supplemented by His life in harmony with the teaching, would prove the teaching of divine origin and Jesus from God. This is the theme of this chapter.

John presents the teaching of Jesus and His relation to the teaching in five clearly defined areas: (1) His teaching concerning sin and His relation to sin; (2) His teaching concerning law and His relation to law; (3) His teaching concerning the kingdom and His relation to the kingdom in which the law operates; (4) His teaching concerning man and His relation to man, the creature who has violated the law and is therefore under sin; and (5) His teaching concerning God and His relation to God, who seeks to save man from sin and to give him a place in the kingdom.

Simply stated, the issue is this: all wrong conduct is in the violation of law. But back of law is the kingdom in which that law operates. That kingdom is made up of men, animals, vegetation, or forces, which are subject to the law, who either comply with it or disobey it. Back of those who make up the kingdom is the final and supreme Being or Force to whom all are responsible. It is the purpose of this chapter to show that in His relation to sin, to the law, to violation of the law, to the kingdom in which the law operates, to man, who is the subject of the kingdom, and to God, who is the Creator and source of all, Jesus maintained a perfect relation in every way.

SIN.
Jesus' Teaching Concerning Sin and His Relation to Sin

Sin is defined as "a missing the mark, transgression, unrighteousness, impiety, contempt and violation of law, depravity, desire for what is forbidden (lust)."[1] It is readily recognized that its root idea is that of missing the mark toward which one should aim, the transgression and violation of law which one should honor. Jesus' teaching concerning sin and the sinner and His own relation to sin set Him apart from men as one unique in every respect.

Jesus' attitude toward the sinner is well illustrated by the mercy He showed toward the woman taken in adultery. The Pharisees brought her to Him for judgment, but they were not concerned with the woman or her lot; they sought only an occasion whereby they might accuse Jesus. Their charge was that she had been taken in the act of adultery and that the law of Moses commanded such a one be stoned. They tried to put Him in a dilemma by asking, "What do you say?" When pressed for a reply, the Lord said, "He that is without sin among you, let him first cast a stone at her" (8:7). He had been writing on the ground, and after this challenge He continued to write. A part of the law overlooked by these hypocrites was, "The hand of the witnesses shall be first upon him to put him to death, and afterward the hand of all the people" (Deut. 17:7). When they heard Jesus' charge, they went out one by one, beginning with the eldest among them. No one was willing to cast the first stone. When all had gone and Jesus was left alone with the woman, He asked, "Woman, where are they? did no man condemn thee?" To this she replied, "No man, Lord." Jesus' answer was one of mercy to the sinner, but it was not an indication of indifference to the sin, when He said, "Neither do I condemn thee: go thy way; from henceforth sin no more" (8:1-11).

This incident was followed by a heated discussion between Jesus and the Jerusalem Jews concerning sin and varied aspects of sin. Jesus led into the discussion by saying, "I go away, and ye shall seek me, and shall die in your sin: whither I go, ye cannot come" (8:21). This emphasizes three points: Jesus was going away; whither He should go they could not come; they should die in their sins. Thus sin is the determining factor in their inability to follow Him.

Jesus taught further that everyone who commits sin is the bondservant of sin, that the bondservant abides not in the house

---

1. *ISBE*, "Sin," p. 2798.

but is cast out, and that if the Son should make one free, he should be free indeed (8:34-36). In this Jesus claimed that He had power over sin and that He alone could free one from sin's power.

As the discussion proceeded, Jesus charged that those who commit sin are of the devil, that sin relates one to the devil, and that the devil is the author of sin: "Ye are of your father the devil, and the lusts of your father it is your will to do. He was a murderer from the beginning, and standeth not in the truth, because there is no truth in him. When he speaketh a lie, he speaketh of his own: for he is a liar, and the father thereof" (8:44). This makes several points clear: sin separated the Jews from God so that they could not follow Jesus; sin brought them into bondage; sin is of the devil and thus relates the sinner to the devil.

Jesus then declared His own freedom from sin when He challenged them, "Which of you convicteth me of sin?" (v. 46). No man was able to convict Him. The only reply they could make was one of prejudice, founded upon no evidence; they said, "Say we not well that thou art a Samaritan, and hast a demon?" (v. 48). To this day the challenge of Jesus, "Which of you convicteth me of sin," remains unanswered.

His teaching did not stop with His pointing out the bondage of the sinner and the sinner's impotence to deliver himself from this bondage. Jesus proposed to provide for the sinner's deliverance from bondage by the sacrifice of Himself for sin. He taught that in the erecting of the brazen serpent by Moses there was a type of His being lifted up. He said, "as Moses lifted up the serpent in the wilderness, even so must the Son of man be lifted up; that whosoever believeth may in him have eternal life" (3:14, 15). Under the allegory of "bread" Jesus taught, "I am the living bread which came down out of heaven: if any man eat of this bread, he shall live for ever; yea and the bread which I will give is my flesh, for the life of the world" (6:51). Under the allegory of the shepherd and his sheep, Jesus said, "I am the good shepherd: the good shepherd layeth down his life for the sheep . . . And I lay down my life for the sheep" (10:11, 15). Then, as He drew toward the close of His life, He further disclosed, "Now is the judgment of this world: now shall the prince of this world be cast out. And I, if I be lifted up from the earth, will draw all men unto myself. But this he said, signifying by what manner of death he should die" (12:31-33).

Jesus was perfect in His relation to sin; He had a complete understanding of sin in its origin, the consequence of sin, and that which was necessary to free man from its bondage. Though He recognized Himself as being without sin, He always showed mercy toward the sinner and taught that He would be the sacrifice which would free man from sin. This sacrifice was completed on the cross, where He accomplished the purpose for which He had come into the world. He closed His life with the words, "It is finished" (19:28-30).

LAW.
Jesus' Teaching
Concerning the Law
and His Relation
to the Law

Back of sin is the law; violation of the law is sin. What is Jesus' teaching concerning that law? What is His relation to the law? Here again is found perfect harmony between teaching and life. Jesus taught that "the law," "the word of God," and "the scripture" are equivalent expressions. When accused of blasphemy "because that thou, being a man, makest thyself God," Jesus replied, "Is it not written in your *law*, I said, Ye are gods? If he called them gods, unto whom *the word of God* came (and *the scripture* cannot be broken), say ye of him, whom the Father sanctified and sent into the world, Thou blasphemest; because I said, I am the Son of God?" (10:34-36). Inasmuch as the law is here called "the word of God," it follows that God is the giver of the law. But Jesus claimed, "I and the Father are one" (10:30), which ascribed to Himself equality with and perfect relation to the Father, the giver of the law.

Jesus claimed that in His teaching He was spokesman for God in revealing God and His new law: "My teaching is not mine, but his that sent me"; "as the Father taught me, I speak these things"; "For I spake not from myself; but the Father that sent me, he hath given me a commandment, what I should say, and what I should speak" (7:16; 8:28; 12:49. See also 5:19; 14:23, 24; 15:10; etc.). Further, He claimed the right to give a new law when He said, "A new commandment I give unto you" (13:34).

In summary of His teaching concerning the law, Jesus taught that the law was God's law, that He was one with God, that He was God's spokesman to man, and that as such He had the right to give a new commandment. His challenge to His enemies, "Which of you convicteth me of sin?" would apply equally to the violation of His own teaching as well as to the violation of the law which they recognized. Which one among you convicts me of breaking either the law you call God's law or the teaching which I bring to you? This is the solemn invitation of Jesus to investigate His life in the light of both. Perfection in His concept and teaching concerning His relation to God, the giver of law, and His keeping the law which was given is again clearly revealed.

KINGDOM.
Jesus' Teaching
Concerning the Kingdom
and His Relation
to the Kingdom

Back of law there is a kingdom in which that law operates, whether the kingdom is physical, political, moral, or spiritual. Inasmuch as God is Spirit and laws that pertain to man's relation to Him are spiritual, there must be a spiritual kingdom in which those laws operate. What is the teaching of Jesus concerning that kingdom? What is His relation to the kingdom? Here again one finds the same perfection of teaching and relationship that he found above.

When arraigned before Pilate and charged with being a rival to Caesar, Jesus affirmed the spiritual nature of the kingdom when He denied that His kingdom was of this world. In answer to Pilate's question, "What hast thou done?" Jesus replied, "My kingdom is not of this world: if my kingdom were of this world, then would my servants fight, that I should not be delivered to the Jews: but now is my kingdom not from hence" (18:35-36). The kingdom of which He spoke and of which He taught, being not of this world, could not be defended by the sword. There was therefore no competition between Jesus and Pilate, between His kingdom and that of Caesar.

Pilate proceeded with the examination by asking, "Art thou a king then?" To this Jesus replied, "Thou sayest that I am a king. To this end have I been born, and to this end am I come into the world, that I should bear witness unto the truth. Every one that is of the truth heareth my voice" (v. 37). He was a king, but not in competition with Pilate or Caesar; He and they were kings of different worlds. His kingdom was a kingdom of truth, to be established, perpetuated, and extended by truth. It was to this end that Jesus had come into the world. The entire period of His brief life, beginning with His baptism, had been dedicated to the task of revealing the truth and of persuading men to accept it. The truth that He taught was spiritual truth; the kingdom which He sought to establish was a spiritual kingdom, in which that truth should operate. Pilate's reply, "What is truth?" indicates an interest in that truth which Jesus taught, a desire to know the truth concerning Jesus that he might more accurately judge Him, or contempt for such a king and kingdom. It is not ours to judge the motive that prompted Pilate's question. However, we know that he was not fair with the evidence he had, for three times he declared, "I find no crime in him," only to reverse the judgment and turn Jesus over to the Jews to be crucified. It seems that he had little or no interest in spiritual truth.

The teaching of Jesus before Pilate was consistent with His teaching throughout His ministry. To Nicodemus He had taught that entrance into the kingdom was by a spiritual birth, "Verily, verily, I say unto thee, Except one be born of water and the Spirit, he cannot enter into the kingdom of God. That which is born of the flesh is flesh; and that which is born of the Spirit is spirit. Marvel not that I said unto thee, Ye must be born anew" (3:5-7). Man is born into the physical world by a physical birth and thereby becomes subject to physical laws. He is born under some form of civil rule, thereby becomes subject to a political government under a human ruler. One enters the kingdom of which Christ taught by a spiritual birth through the truth, of which He came to bear witness. Thus man becomes subject to spiritual law and under a spiritual king. The word of God—spiritual truth— pertains to a spiritual kingdom.

This conversation with Nicodemus was followed by Jesus' conversation with the Samaritan woman, in which He taught her that the worship of God should be a spiritual worship. In answer to her statement, "Our fathers worshipped in this mountain; and ye say, that in Jerusalem is the place where men ought to worship" (4:20), Jesus cut the tap root of localized worship and proceeded to lay deep the foundation of true worship. First, Jesus cleared the question of "place" when He said, "Woman, believe me, the hour cometh, when neither in this mountain, nor in Jerusalem, shall ye worship the Father" (v. 21). The place is indifferent, but the object and character of worship are deeply significant. He made this clear as He continued, "the hour cometh, and now is, when the true worshippers shall worship the Father (the object of true worship) in spirit (the character of true worship) and truth (the standard of true worship): for such doth the Father seek to be his worshippers. God is a Spirit: and they that worship him must worship in spirit and truth" (4:23, 24).

The nature of the kingdom was emphasized earlier in His ministry when Jesus refused the crown they would have bestowed upon Him. When the multitude in Galilee had sought to take Him by force and make Him king, He had dismissed the people and withdrawn into the mountain to be alone (6:15). Had His kingdom been temporal in its nature, He would have encouraged them in the thing they tried to do. But because His kingdom is spiritual in its nature, He followed their effort with the sermon on the bread of life, in which He sifted the multitude to determine whether they would accept a spiritual Messiah ruling over a spiritual kingdom. The sermon proved to be a "hard saying"; so upon hearing it, "many of his disciples went back, and walked no more with him" (6:66). They were not ready for the kind of kingdom He had come to establish.

In His preparation for death and His going away, Jesus endeavored to prepare His disciples for the event by making clear to them that as citizens of His kingdom they would not be of this world. In the private conversation with them at the last supper, after Judas had gone out from their midst, Jesus taught that in their relation to Him they were as branches in a vine (15:1-11). In their relation to one another as believers, they were to "love one another, even as I have loved you," bearing fruit that should abide (15:12-17). In their relation to the world, He said, "If ye were of the world, the world would love its own; but because ye are not of the world, but I chose you out of the world, therefore the world hateth you" (15:19). This point is further emphasized in His prayer to the Father, when He said, "The world hated them, because they are not of the world, even as I am not of the world" (17:14); and again, "They are not of the world, even as I am not of the world" (v. 16).

In His teaching Jesus emphasized clearly that the kingdom is not of this world, but that it is a kingdom of truth. It is entered by a spiritual birth, and its citizens worship in spirit and truth. As citizens of His kingdom, they are not of this world. He taught that He is the founder of the kingdom, the king of the kingdom, and that it is strictly a kingdom not of this world, but of truth. His life was lived in perfect harmony with this ideal. He put no emphasis on money as a vital part of the kingdom. He repudiated force as an element in the founding or perpetuating of the kingdom when He said to Peter, "Put up the sword into the sheath" (18:11). The sword had no place in His plan. Also, He put no emphasis on the founding of schools, the erecting of buildings, or the control of territory, for these likewise had no place in His kingdom.

He appealed to no inducement to follow Him except love for truth and moral principles of right, and for those blessings which would grow out of truth. He promised them that He would make provision for them and that they would be with Him (14:1-3). He would pray the Father that He send the Holy Spirit to them, who should abide with them (14:16-17). Through the truth He spoke, His joy would be in them (15:11). In the truth that He spoke, they would find peace (14:27; 16:33). In the world they would have tribulation, for tribulation would follow them in their discipleship and in their stand against the world; but they could be of good cheer, for He had overcome the world (16:33). At no time did He seek for Himself or promise to His disciples anything material, sensual, or physical as a part of His kingdom. The things of the world, which appeal to the lust of the flesh, the lust of the eye, or the pride of life, are wholly lacking in His efforts to gain men. There is perfect integration between His teaching and His life. What He taught He lived, and what He eliminated from His teaching in the building of His kingdom He avoided in His own life. His teaching and life stand as an aspect of His moral glory, which testifies to His being the Son of God.

MAN.
Jesus' Teaching
Concerning Man
and His Relation
to Men

The kingdom is a spiritual kingdom; however, it is a kingdom composed of men, not of angels or disembodied spirits. Again the teaching of Jesus and His own conduct in relation to that teaching are so related that they point to His being man as other men, yet more than a man.

Jesus related Himself to man as a member of the human family (*anthropos,* a human being, without reference to sex), when He said, "But now ye seek to kill me, a *man* that hath told you the truth" (8:40). He displayed various characteristics of all men as when, "being wearied with his journey," He sat by the well as the disciples went into the village to buy food (4:6). He displayed the human disposition to weep with those who weep, sharing with them a common feeling of sympathy as He wept before the tomb of Lazarus (11:35). From the cross He said, "I thirst" (19:28), thus identifying Himself with the common appetites and needs of the human race.

Yet Jesus detached Himself from man; He kept Himself distinct from man. Man was in darkness (3:18-20), but He was "the light of the world" (8:12). Only God was the object of true worship (4:23ff.), but He accepted worship (9:38). In Himself as the Son of Man was revealed a relation to the entire human family, while at the same time in Him was to be seen the Father's perfect ideal for man which God would have every man to be. After the resurrection His instruction was, "Go unto my brethren, and say to them, I ascend unto my Father and your Father, and my God and your God" (20:17). This clear distinction between Himself and others was never lost sight of. Jesus knew what was in man; He was man in every sense of the word, yet He was distinct from man. The harmony between His teaching and the revelation of His own life in relation to that teaching confirms His claim to be both man and God.

GOD.
Jesus' Teaching
Concerning God
and His Relation
to God

Back of the kingdom composed of men is God, the one to whom man is related by creation, separated by sin, and accountable to as a creature, and to whom he must be returned. Since the claims of Jesus in His relation to God have been discussed in

Chapter 2, allusion to that teaching will be brief, with the added thought that His life was in every way in keeping with and worthy of the things He taught.

Jesus claimed that He knew God, because He had come from Him, and that God had sent Him (7:29). He "came down out of heaven" (6:38). He was one with God (10:30). He taught that to see and know Him is to see and know the Father (14:7-10); and that life eternal is in this knowledge of the Father and Son (17:3). He claimed glory with the Father before the world was, hence, that He was co-existent with the Father (17:5), that He would return to the Father (16:10, 17, 28), and that He is the way, the only way, to the Father (14:6).

When one studies the life of Jesus, he sees nothing in that life out of harmony with the claims that He made concerning His knowledge of God or with His relation to Him. His relation with the Father was one of perfection; His life betrayed no flaw that would reflect upon the claim. His knowledge of God was absolute; His teaching was truth; His conduct was in every point harmonious with that truth. The attributes of the Father as set forth in His teaching are attributes that one finds in Jesus' own life. When one has seen Jesus, he feels that truly he has seen the Father; and as he listens to His teaching, he becomes convinced that His teaching is not of man, but of God.

Conclusion

This leads one to ask how the four evangelists solved this mighty problem of deity and humanity. Whence came the picture of such a one whose teaching and life are in such perfect harmony? There can be but one rational answer. They had before them the personal and historic Christ whose relation to all things was one of perfection. This perfect relation was one of sinlessness to sin, of obedience to law, of founder to the kingdom in which the law operates, of kinship to man, who must be fitted for the kingdom, and of oneness with God, whose is the law and kingdom. There is only one logical answer: they had before them both Him and the teaching of Him of whom they wrote, and they wrote of Him by the Holy Spirit.

The Holy Spirit's Testimony

10

More is said in the Gospel of John about the Holy Spirit—of His person, character, coming, work, and witness—than in any of the other Gospels. As the day of His death drew near, Jesus endeavored to prepare the disciples for it by the things He said in the long conversation with them recorded in chapters 14-16. The discourse was delivered after He ate the last supper with them and after Judas departed (ch. 13), and was followed by His prayer addressed to the Father and sometimes referred to as His "high priestly" prayer (ch. 17).

Two phases of the Spirit's work are considered in this chapter: (1) the mission of the Spirit, as promised by Jesus, and (2) the witness of the Spirit, that is, His testimony to the deity of Christ. The testimony of the Holy Spirit to the deity of Jesus completes the testimony of the Godhead. The Father bare testimony through the signs or miraculous works, through Old Testament Scripture fulfilled in Jesus, and by the resurrection of Jesus from the dead. Jesus' testimony was in His teaching and the harmony of His life with the teaching, which we have called "His Moral Glory." The testimony of the Holy Spirit, as will be pointed out, is in the completed revelation of truth. The presentation of this testimony takes us outside the Book of John, for the Spirit was not sent until Jesus ascended to the Father. It was in the Spirit's work from Pentecost on that He has borne witness. The coming of the Spirit was contingent on the ascension of Jesus, hence will be added proof that Jesus was raised from the dead.

In order to have a clear understanding of the work of the Spirit as set forth in chapters 14-16, there is one point that first should be made clear. The things said in the chapters were spoken to the apostles, not to all disciples. It was while He was eating the last supper with the twelve that Jesus announced that one of them should betray Him (13:21). Jesus then indicated to Peter who it would be by giving the sop to Judas Iscariot. Upon receiving it, Judas "went out straightway: and it was night" (13:30).

Left alone with the eleven, Jesus began to speak freely of His immediate going away and to prepare them for His departure. It was to these eleven that He gave the word that the Father had given to Him (17:8, 14), and it was to these that He promised the Holy Spirit, who should be with them in His stead and who should guide them into the truth. It should be borne in mind that these promises of the Holy Spirit and the work He should do in guiding into all truth and in bearing witness were promises to the apostles, not to all men.

The mission of the Holy Spirit

1. He was to be with the apostles as a "Comforter"

In this discourse with the eleven, Jesus said, "And I will pray the Father, and he shall give you another Comforter, that he may be with you for ever, even the Spirit of truth: whom the world cannot receive; for it beholdeth him not, neither knoweth him: ye know him; for he abideth with you, and shall be in you. I will not leave you desolate: I come unto you" (14:16-18). Jesus uses the word *Comforter* (*paraklētos*) four times in this discourse, and each time He uses it of the Holy Spirit. In their recently published lexicon, Arndt and Gingrich say of the word, "In the few places where the word is found in pre-Christian and extra-Christian literature it has for the most part a more general meaning: *one*

who appears in another's behalf, mediator, intercessor, helper."[1]
With reference to the interpreters of John's Gospel, these same
writers continue, "In our literature the active sense helper, intercessor is suitable in all occurrences of the word."

Before deducing a conclusion with respect to Jesus' use of the
word *Comforter,* the word *another* should be noted. Vine says,
"*allos* (another) expresses a numerical difference and denotes
another of the same sort" (W. E. Vine). In this case Jesus' use of
"another" indicates that the Comforter being sent would be with
them in the stead of Jesus: "I will pray the Father, and he shall
give you *another* Comforter," one of the same sort as Jesus had
been while He was with them. This is also inferred when Jesus
said, "I will not leave you desolate: I come unto you" (v. 18). His
coming would be in the person of the Holy Spirit.

This indication that the Holy Spirit would be with them as an
aider, succorer, or helper in the stead of Christ is further designated by His words, "These things have I spoken unto you, while
yet abiding with you. But the Comforter, even the Holy Spirit,
whom the Father *will send in my name,* he shall teach you all
things, and bring to your remembrance all that I said unto you"
(vv. 25, 26). Jesus had taught them while with them, but now in
His personal absence the Holy Spirit would both teach and bring
to their remembrance the things Jesus had taught them. This
aspect of His work is discussed below under 4. As Christ had come
in the name of His Father, as one with God and in the stead of
God, so the Holy Spirit would come in Christ's name, as one with
Christ to be with them in the stead of Christ.

These words of assurance were spoken to the apostles when
Jesus promised that the Holy Spirit would abide with them and
would be in them. The conclusion is that the Holy Spirit, whom
the Father would send in answer to the petition of Christ, would
be with and in the apostles as an aider, helper, and succorer in the
stead of Jesus, who would have returned to the Father. They
would not be left desolate.

2. He was to bear witness

The hatred manifested toward Jesus by the Jews was inexcus-
able. Jesus said, "If I had not come and spoken unto them, they

---

1. p. 623.

had not had sin: but now they have no excuse for their sin"
(15:22). He followed this by saying, "If I had not done among
them the works which none other did, they had not had sin: but
now have they both seen and hated both me and my Father"
(v. 24). The words of Jesus' teaching and the works (signs) which
He had done among them left them without excuse for the sin of
unbelief and for their hatred of Him and the Father. But in this
unbelief and hatred they were fulfilling the prophecy, "They hated
me without a cause" (v. 25; Ps. 69:4). Jesus followed this charge
with another promise of the Comforter and a statement of His
mission: "But when the Comforter is come, whom I will send unto
you from the Father, even the Spirit of truth, which proceedeth
from the Father, he shall bear witness of me" (15:26).

As pointed out by Jesus in the continuation of the discourse,
the witness of the Spirit would be threefold. He would convict the
world; He would guide the apostles into all the truth; and He
would glorify Jesus by taking the things that pertained to Him and
declaring them unto the apostles (16:7-14). Inasmuch as the thesis
of this chapter is the witness of the Spirit, a discussion of the
testimony of the Spirit follows.

3. He was to convict the world

As a part of the mission of the Holy Spirit, Jesus introduced
next His work of convicting the world, "And he, when he is come,
will convict the world in respect of sin, and of righteousness, and
of judgment" (16:8). The verb *elegxei,* translated "show him his
fault," "convince," "reprove," and "rebuke," is so elastic as to be
difficult of exact definition. Hendriksen gives a complete list of
the translations of the word in each passage of the New Testament
as it is found in the Authorized, American Standard, and Revised
American Standard versions. He adds that "Moulton and Milligan,
on this verb, prefers the translation *convict* (in the sense of 'bring
to light the true character of a man and his conduct') for all three
instances of its use in the Fourth Gospel."[2] Alford says that as
used here, the word has a double sense, "of a *convincing* unto
salvation, and a *convicting* unto condemnation."[3] Dods says sim-

---

2. Hendriksen, Vol. II, p. 325.
3. Alford, Vol. I, p. 815.

ply, "The verb *elegxei* expresses the idea of pressing home a conviction."[4] The probable meaning of Jesus is that the Holy Spirit will press home a conviction which will convince those disposed to believe, leading to belief, and that He will convict those not so disposed, bringing them under the condemnation of their guilt of rejecting Him and the evidence submitted.

He would convict of sin, "because they believe not on me" (16:9). In spite of the testimony that Jesus came from God, as witnessed by the words spoken and the work done (15:22, 24), the world rejected Him. The work of the Spirit would be to convince them of error and to convict them of the sin of rejecting the Son of God.

He would convict the world of righteousness, "because I go to the Father, and ye behold me no more" (v. 10). In its unbelief the world not only rejected Jesus, but it also had charged Him with breaking the sabbath, with making Himself equal with God, with being possessed with a demon, with blasphemy, with setting Himself up against Caesar as king, and with saying He would destroy the temple and raise it again in three days. His resurrection and return to the Father, from whom would come the Spirit, would convince them of His righteousness and convict them of the sin of false accusation. His righteousness would be vindicated.

The Spirit would convict the world of judgment because in the exaltation of Jesus the judgment of Satan would be demonstrated. The prince of this world would be dethroned from the place he had thus far held over the hearts of men.

4. He was to guide the apostles into all the truth

Jesus had assured the apostles that the Holy Spirit, whom the Father would send in His name, "shall teach you all things, and bring to your remembrance all that I said unto you" (14:26). He would both teach and bring to remembrance. He now sums up this aspect of the Spirit's work in a more emphatic and all-inclusive statement as He says, "I have yet many things to say unto you, but ye cannot bear them now. Howbeit when he, the Spirit of truth, is come, he shall guide you into all the truth" (16:12, 13). It is at this point that the Spirit is bearing witness today. One may

---

4. Dods, Vol. I, p. 835.

defend his unbelief of the "signs" on the ground that he has never seen one, but a critical examination of the completeness of truth as revealed by the Spirit may be made by anyone at any time. It is in this testimony of completed revelation of God's purpose and will, begun in the Old Testament and consummated in Jesus, that the Spirit's strongest testimony lies.

As further testimony of the Spirit, Jesus said, "And he shall declare unto you the things that are to come" (v. 13b). This the Spirit did as He brought to their remembrance the words of Jesus relative to the destruction of Jerusalem (Matt. 24), which was fulfilled in 70 A.D. at the hand of the Romans. He declared the "falling away" which should precede the revealing of "the man of sin" (II Thess. 2:1-7); this falling away began during and continued after Paul's day until the "man of sin" was revealed. The Spirit told that the Roman Empire and its paganism would eventually fall, never to rise again (Book of Revelation); this was accomplished by 476 A.D. He also declared the eventual return of Christ, the resurrection of the dead, the judgment, and the destiny of all men (heaven or hell). These are yet to be fulfilled; but the confidence of the believer that they will be fulfilled rests on evidence of fulfilled prophecies of the Old Covenant and the fulfilled declarations of the Holy Spirit mentioned above.

5. He was to glorify Christ

The whole work of the Holy Spirit was to have been the glorifying of Jesus Christ. "He shall glorify me: for he shall take of mine, and shall declare it unto you" (16:14). From the day of Pentecost, when men began to act under the influence of the Spirit, everything taught or done, in word or deed, was to the end that Christ should be glorified. The work of Jesus Christ in redemption and His fulfilling the eternal purpose of God was the theme of the Spirit. Christ as exalted King and Lord, His authority in the kingdom of God, and His reign in the kingdom of men were heralded by the Spirit through the apostles. His return, the resurrection of the dead, the judgment of all men and ultimate destiny of all were preached to the glory of Christ. The Spirit activated the apostles and led the saints, but the Spirit was never the theme of apostolic preaching. Christ was the center of the entire spiritual system.

The Spirit's Testimony

The coming of the Holy Spirit is additional testimony to the resurrection of Jesus. Jesus had repeatedly claimed that He came from the Father and that He would return to Him from whom He had come. To the Jews in Jerusalem, He had said, "I go unto him that sent me" (7:33). To the eleven at supper, He had said of the believer, "and greater works than these shall he do; because I go unto the Father" (14:12). When discussing with them His going away, He said, "If ye loved me, ye would have rejoiced, because I go unto the Father" (14:28). And now, as He prepared them for His going away by giving them final instructions concerning the work of the Spirit, He said, "But now I go unto him that sent me" (16:5). In these statements He had clearly testified that He would go away, that He would go to the Father.

But between His active ministry among them and His going away there would be His resurrection. When He had spoken to the Jews of their destroying "this temple, and in three days I will raise it up" (2:19), Jesus had spoken of the resurrection of His body. In the discussion of Himself as the good shepherd, He had said, "I lay down my life, that I may take it again" (10:11, 17). His death and resurrection would precede His going away—His going to the Father.

When Jesus therefore said, "Nevertheless I tell you the truth: It is expedient for you that I go away; for if I go not away, the Comforter will not come unto you; but if I go, I will send him unto you" (16:7), He was saying that the coming of the Holy Spirit was contingent on His going away. He does not explain why; He simply states the fact. But His going was contingent on His resurrection. Therefore, if the Spirit came, Jesus had been raised from the dead and had returned to the Father. This is further indicated in references to His glory.

The coming of the Holy Spirit was to follow Jesus' entrance into His glory. Jesus had spoken of rivers of living water flowing from within the believer; John adds, "But this spake he of the Spirit, which they that believed on him were to receive: for the Spirit was not yet given; because Jesus was not yet glorified" (7:39). The Spirit, according to this, was not to be given until Jesus should be glorified. John says of the entrance of Jesus into the city and of the loud acclamations of the people that the disciples did not understand these things at the first, "but when Jesus was glorified, then remembered they" (12:16). Shortly thereafter the Greeks came to Philip with the request that they, too, would see Jesus. When Philip and Andrew brought the request to Jesus, He said, "The hour is come, that the Son of man should be glorified" (12:23). At the last supper, after Judas had left the group, Jesus said, "Now is the Son of man glorified, and God is glorified in him; and God shall glorify him in himself, and straightway shall he glorify him" (13:31-32). In His prayer to the Father immediately before His betrayal, He said, "Father, the hour is come; glorify thy Son, that the Son may glorify thee" (17:1), followed with the petition, "And now, Father, glorify thou me with thine own self with the glory which I had with thee before the world was" (v. 5). These passages point to the resurrection of Jesus and beyond this event to His entrance into His glory with the Father. After the resurrection He told Mary to say to His brethren, "I ascend unto my Father and your Father, and my God and your God" (20:17).

The point is this: the Spirit was not to come until Jesus should be glorified. Jesus was not glorified until after His death and resurrection and His return to the Father. Therefore, the Spirit could not come until after He had been raised from the dead and had returned to Him from whom He had come. The Spirit could not come until Jesus should go away, but His going away was dependent on His resurrection from the dead. Therefore, the coming of the Spirit would be witness to the fact that Jesus was raised from the dead and had entered into His glory.

At this point in discussing the witness of the Spirit in the complete revelation of truth, it is necessary to go beyond the Book of John. The Holy Spirit did not come until Pentecost, fifty days after the resurrection; hence His work was after the close of the Book of John and took up where Jesus left off. At this point we move to the work of the Spirit, which begins where the Gospel of John ends.

1. The mystery is revealed

Jesus used the word *mystery* only once. When He began to speak in parables, He answered the disciples' question, "Why do you speak in parables?" by saying, "Unto you it is given to know the mysteries of the kingdom of heaven (of God)" (Matt. 13:11; Mark 4:11; Luke 8:10). However, the word *mystery* was a favorite with Paul; he uses it twenty times in his epistles. Aside from the one time Jesus used it and the many times Paul used it, only John used the word; it is found four times in the Book of Revelation.

Our English word is a transliteration of the Greek *mustērion,* which is defined as *"secret, secret rite, secret teaching, mystery,* a religious technical term applied in secular Greek (predominantly plural) mostly to the mysteries with their secret teachings, religious and political in nature, concealed within many strange customs and ceremonies."[5] Of its use in the New Testament, Thayer says, "In the scriptures, 1) a hidden or secret thing not obvious to the understanding. . . 2) a hidden purpose or counsel; secret will. . . In the New Testament, God's plan of providing salvation for men through Christ, which was once hidden, but now is revealed."[6] A mystery, "For this cause I Paul, the prisoner of Christ Jesus in which cannot be comprehended until it is revealed. The Greek mystery religions were known only to the initiated. The things of God's divine purpose are understood and known only as God has revealed them.

The work of the Holy Spirit, which was to guide the apostles into all the truth, would be to reveal through the apostles the secret things of God's eternal purpose and that which Christ had accomplished in His teaching and ministry. The gospel as preached and taught by the apostles is the revealing of the mystery—God's purpose hidden from before the foundation of the world.

Paul makes clear the fact that the Holy Spirit has revealed the mystery, "For this cause I Paul, the prisoner of Christ Jesus in behalf of you Gentiles,—if so be that ye have heard of the dispensation of that grace of God which was given me to you-ward; how that by revelation was made known unto me the mystery, as I wrote before in few words, whereby, when ye read, ye can perceive my understanding in the mystery of Christ; which in other generations was not made known unto the sons of men, as it hath now been revealed unto his holy apostles and prophets in the Spirit" (Eph. 3:1-5). Several points impress us: (1) The dispensation of grace, which should include the Gentiles on the same basis with the Jews, was "a mystery," something not understood

---

5. Arndt and Gingrich, pp. 531-532.
6. Thayer, p. 420.

or made known. (2) It is now revealed, not discovered, because it was beyond the pale of man's ability to discover. (3) It was revealed by the Holy Spirit. (4) We can understand Paul's understanding when we read that which he understood; therefore, that which was revealed to the apostles was for us also. (5) Since we can understand by reading, we do not need an inspired teacher or a hierarchy to interpret for us.

To the Corinthians Paul affirmed that the gospel, as a mystery, has been revealed through the Spirit (I Cor. 2:6-13). He impresses these points: (1) The wisdom which the apostles spoke was a wisdom not of this world. (2) It was God's wisdom in a mystery, even the wisdom that had been hidden, which God had foreordained before the worlds. (3) It was a mystery which none of the rulers of the world had known. (4) The things which God had prepared for man, unknown to man, were now being revealed through the Spirit, who searches all things, even the deep things of God. (5) A man can understand the things of a man only as the spirit of a man makes these things known. (6) So also the things of God can be known only as the Spirit of God reveals them. (7) But the Spirit received by the apostles was the Spirit of God. (8) The Spirit of God had taken the things of God and made them known to the apostles, combining these spiritual things with spiritual words—that is, choosing the words through which the things of God were made known.

The complete revealing of God's purpose, which in times past had been unknown—a mystery—is the Spirit's witness to the deity of Christ, guiding the apostles into all truth, as Jesus had said He would.

2. The grace of God has been made known

When the Word became flesh we beheld His glory, says John, "full of grace and truth. . . . For of his fulness we all received, and grace for grace. For the law was given through Moses; grace and truth came through Jesus Christ" (John 1:14, 16-17). Paul says, "For the grace of God hath appeared, bringing salvation to all men," instructing us how to live and for what to look (Titus 2:11-14).

Grace (*charis*) may be defined "as favor out of good will,"[7] or as "kindness which bestows upon one what he had not deserved."[8] It is favor which one does not deserve or merit. The coming of Jesus into the world to free man from sin and to redeem him unto God was an act of kindness on God's part, undeserved and unmerited by man.

The Spirit's work was to guide the apostles into all truth concerning this grace. Peter writes, "Concerning which salvation (i.e., the salvation of your souls [v. 9]) the prophets sought and searched diligently, who prophesied of the grace that should come unto you" (I Peter 1:10). The theme of the prophets was the grace that should come to those of Peter's day and of ours. "Searching what time or what manner of time the Spirit of Christ which was in them did point unto, when it testified beforehand the sufferings of Christ, and the glories that should follow them" (v. 11). The prophets, by the same Spirit of Christ which He promised the apostles, pointed to and testified of the sufferings of Christ and the glories that should follow the sufferings. "To whom (i.e., the prophets) it was revealed, that not unto themselves, but unto you, did they minister these things, which now have been announced unto you through them that preached the gospel unto you by the Holy Spirit sent forth from heaven; which things angels desire to look into" (v. 12). Peter says that it was the Holy Spirit who was now making known this grace of salvation through the preaching of the gospel by the apostles.

It was by the same Spirit that the grace was written for preservation unto all generations. Peter concluded his epistle by saying, "By Silvanus, our faithful brother, as I account him, I have written unto you briefly, exhorting, and testifying that this is the true grace of God: stand ye fast therein" (I Peter 5:12).

The argument is that the Spirit should guide the apostles into all the truth, revealing it through them. The grace of God appeared, bringing salvation. The Spirit, through the apostles, announced or made known that grace, and by the same Spirit the grace was written. The conclusion is that the Spirit did the work He was to do: He revealed the truth of the grace of God, and through Peter and the other apostles He wrote it for all generations to come.

---

7. Arndt and Gingrich, p. 885.
8. Thayer, p. 666.

3. The faith has been once for all delivered

Peter addresses his second epistle to "them that have obtained a like precious faith with us in the righteousness of our God and the Saviour Jesus Christ" (II Peter 1:1). By this it is understood that the faith of the saints was the same as that of the apostles, "a like precious faith."

Whatever Jude had purposed beforehand to write, he begins the body of his epistle by saying, "Beloved, while I was giving all diligence to write unto you of our common salvation, I was constrained to write unto you exhorting you to contend earnestly for the faith which was once for all delivered unto the saints" (Jude 3). Jude's "common salvation" is the basis of Peter's "like precious faith." Jude's "the faith" is the body of doctrine as revealed by the Spirit. Luke says, "and a great company of the priests were obedient to the faith" (Acts 6:7). Jude's declaration that it was "once for all delivered" is his affirmation that it is complete, not to be repeated or to be added to; it is final. That it was "delivered" means it was revealed, not discovered. It was "delivered" by the Holy Spirit as He revealed it to the apostles. "To the saints" makes the saints the trustees of the faith; it was not delivered to a special hierarchy or to a select "clergy" but to the saints. It is theirs to understand, to practice, and to rely upon; they need no hierarchy to interpret it to them.

Since the apostles completed their work, not one line has been added to the faith once for all delivered. This is the Spirit's testimony to the omniscience, truthfulness, and deity of Jesus.

4. Man is made a partaker of the divine nature

Peter continues, saying to those who had obtained "a like precious faith" with the apostles, "Grace to you and peace be multiplied in the knowledge of God and of Jesus our Lord; seeing that His divine power hath granted unto us all things that pertain unto life and godliness, through the knowledge of him that called us by his own glory and virtue" (II Peter 1:2-3). The "divine power" is that power of God wrought in Christ when He raised Him from the dead (Eph. 1:20); this power now operates on men through the Holy Spirit as He worked through the apostles. After His resurrection, Jesus had said to the apostles, "And behold, I send forth the promise of my Father upon you: but tarry ye in the city, until ye be clothed with power from on high" (Luke 24:49); and again, "but ye shall receive power, when the Holy Spirit is come upon you" (Acts 1:8). Through the Holy Spirit, God's divine power had granted all things that pertained unto life and godliness and had made the saints partakers of the divine nature.

This partaking of the divine nature was the realization of that which had been promised in the Gospel of John. It had been said of Jesus, "He came unto his own, and they that were his own received him not. But as many as received him, to them gave he the right to become children of God, even to them that believe on his name: who were born, not of blood, nor of the will of the flesh, nor of the will of man, but of God" (John 1:11-13). Jesus referred to this birth "of God" when He said to Nicodemus, "Except one be born of water and the Spirit, he cannot enter into the kingdom of God" (3:5). These born of "the will of God" are these born "of water and the Spirit," who thereby become the children of God. The individual thus born was assured by Jesus that as a believer, from within him (the believer) should "flow rivers of living water. But this spake he of the Spirit, which they that believed on him were to receive" (7:38-39). Further, it was to have been the work of the Spirit to "convict . . . of sin, and of righteousness, and of judgment" (16:8), which should lead to the new birth.

The Holy Spirit was to convict of the sin of unbelief, thus making of the individual a believer, giving him the right or power to become a son of God through the birth of water and the Spirit; thus when he was born, the Spirit should dwell in him, relating him to God as His son. So Peter says that the divine power granted the things pertaining to godliness and that through these things which pertain to godliness man becomes a partaker of the divine nature. But this new birth could come only by the Holy Spirit through the word, and so did come. The transformation of sinners into the likeness of God and their partaking of the divine nature is the Spirit's testimony to the deity of Christ.

5. Men are thoroughly furnished unto every good work

As a newborn son of God, a man can know what good works God would have him do in His service only as God reveals to him what He considers good works. In his second letter to Timothy, Paul wrote, "Every scripture inspired of God is also profitable for teaching, for reproof, for correction, for instruction which is in righteousness: that the man of God may be complete, furnished completely unto every good work" (II Tim. 3:16-17). The King James Version is probably more nearly correct: "all scripture is given by inspiration of God"; that is, all scripture is God-breathed. Scripture provides all that is essential for teaching, imparting knowledge of God and of His will, for reproof, warning and rebuttal of error, for correction of that which has been reproved, and for instruction in righteousness, training in the way of righteousness.

Further, Scripture provides unto every good work. All that comes under the head of "good works" is provided in the sacred writings. Through this provision the man of God, the Christian, is made complete; there is nothing lacking. In order to make the man of God complete, Scripture would have to be complete. Again, the completeness of the revelation of truth, by which the man of God is made complete, is the Spirit's testimony to the deity of Jesus.

Conclusion

Since by the Holy Spirit the mystery is revealed, the grace of God is made known, the faith has been once for all delivered, and man is made partaker of the divine nature and is thoroughly furnished unto every good work, we conclude that all truth is now revealed and is therefore complete. In this completed revelation of truth, the Holy Spirit has borne, and continues to bear, witness that Jesus Christ is the Son of God.

In the face of the evidence, we are left with the decision that Christ's claims are such that either He is the Son of God or He is a blasphemer, a deceiver, an impostor, a hypocrite, and a falsifier; certainly He is not "merely a good man."

The testimony of the Father in the signs done by Jesus, in the Old Testament scriptures fulfilled, and in the resurrection of Jesus and the testimony of the Holy Spirit and His work, as presented in the Gospel of John, is such that belief must follow. As reason weighs the evidence and fits it all together in every part, it can but conclude that Jesus is what He claimed to be and what John claimed for Him; He is the Christ, the Son of the living God!

"Yet They Believed Not on Him"   11

In spite of the overwhelming evidence, "and though he had done so many signs before them," the fact remains, "yet they believed not on him" (12:37). That is, the vast majority of the Jews of Jesus' day and of the generations since have not believed on Him. One can but ask, "Why?" The evidence convinced many then and thousands since, but other millions have remained unimpressed. Is it because the evidence is weak and unconvincing? This cannot be the reason, for the evidence is overwhelming and unanswerable. Or, is the answer to be found in the hearts of those who heard and saw Jesus in person? In looking at the attitudes of those who heard and saw Him yet believed not, one may find the cause for his own unbelief and the reasons why millions today do not believe.

In all fairness to the Jews who rejected the evidence, it can be pointed out that none had the evidence in its fulness, all at one time before him, as it is brought together in the Gospel of John. The situation in Jerusalem and Judea may have been as it would be in our average American city today. If we ask a man whether or not he has heard of Jesus and believes in Him, most likely he will say, "Yes, I have heard of Him," and he either believes or does not believe. But in reality, has he heard of Him? Has the evidence been presented in such abundance and clarity that he can truly say, "I have heard of Him"?

The Jews heard Him teach, they saw His miracles performed, but they did not see the evidence in its fulness as John presents it. Some heard and saw on one occasion, others on different occasions, but they failed to understand the depth and true significance of Jesus' deity. John points out the conditions of heart that caused the Jews not to believe.

No claim is made that the following list of conditions of heart found in the Gospel of John is exhaustive. Others probably could be added, but these are suggested as probable explanations for unbelief in Jesus' time and for unbelief today; human nature and the evidence remain the same.

Superficial or Fickle Belief

When Jesus went up to Jerusalem and cleansed the temple of those who sold animals and birds and of those who exchanged the money of foreign Jews who had come to worship, it is said, "Many believed on his name, beholding his signs which he did" (2:23). But the belief was superficial; it was shallow. The people did not look beneath the surface nor behind the action for the true meaning of Jesus' works.

As the conflict between Jesus and the Jerusalem Jews developed, the unbelief of those Jews became more and more apparent. Finally they were so prevailed upon by the leaders in their city that they asked for the life of Jesus as a traitor, guilty of the highest treason. So aroused were they by the Pharisees that when Jesus was on trial before Pilate they were moved to cry out, "Away with him, away with him, crucify him!" Pilate asked if he should crucify their king, to which the chief priests replied, "We have no king but Caesar" (19:15). Jesus was then delivered up to be crucified. The fickleness of their conviction and the superficial character of their belief made it easy for strong leaders to cause them to reverse themselves completely.

There are always those who are looking for the sensational. In the excitement of emotional pressure, these leave the impression of having conviction; but they are like the tender plant from seed sown in shallow soil. When the excitement is past, the conviction withers and dies. This is another expression of superficial belief. These look for the sensational instead of looking for solid and firm truth. Some in Jesus' day were like that. They were interested in the signs; they were excited about such wonders. They looked for the Messiah to appear in a sensational manner; they were not ready to receive one who had been reared among them and whom they had known. Some of the Jews of Jerusalem said, "Is not this he whom they seek to kill? And lo, he speaketh openly, and they say nothing unto him. Can it be that the rulers indeed know that this is the Christ?" But no sooner had they expressed themselves until they found an answer by which they could dismiss the matter: "Howbeit we know this man whence he is: but when the Christ cometh, no one knoweth whence he is" (7:25-27). A lowly one reared in Nazareth could not be the Christ. Someone more sensational was necessary.

So it is with many today. The spectacular appeals to the multitude; the sensational attracts the shallow-minded. Jesus is too drab. He sought then, and seeks now, to win by the simple teaching of truth. "He shall not cry aloud, neither shall his voice be heard in the street." He was not a rabble-rouser, nor did He appeal to force, to which emotionalism often leads. He rejected the sword as the instrument of establishing, defending, or extending His kingdom. He made no appeal on the ground of greatness. His appeal was not sensational and the motive of emotional sensationalism was completely repudiated. Those looking for such in Him are disappointed.

Lack of Spiritual Perception

Lack of spiritual perception was one of the faults which hindered belief among the common people. It is much the same today. When Jesus had fed the multitude, after having spent the day teaching them, they sought to take Him by force and make Him king (6:15). Jesus followed this by preaching the sermon on the bread of life, in which He strove to make them see that they were not to put the emphasis on the physical but on the spiritual; but they could not comprehend. "This is a hard saying; who can hear it?" was their response. "Upon this many of his disciples went back, and walked no more with him" (6:60, 66).

This condition is seen throughout the Book of John. Lack of spiritual perception hindered then; it hinders today. Too many are looking not for a spiritual Messiah and kingdom, but for that which combines the physical or material with the spiritual. Jesus' kingdom and all that pertains to it is wholly spiritual. It is difficult for men to divorce spiritual from material, but in Christ's teaching they are divorced and must ever remain so. Nicodemus seems to have had difficulty in distinguishing the spiritual from the material. From the conversation between him and Jesus, one perceives his difficulty in grasping a clear distinction between the spiritual and the temporal nature of the kingdom (John 3). His years of background, teaching, and expectation had dulled his spiritual perception and focused his hope on a politically oriented temporal kingdom. He recognized the signs, but he could not see the spiritual significance of what Jesus was doing. However, this weak beginning of faith appears to have grown stronger through the months that followed (cf. 7:50-51; 19:38-40), but to what ultimate fruition we are not told.

Oftentimes an intimacy that takes for granted or an association that makes an acquaintance commonplace hinders spiritual perception. This may portray a shallow vein in people's thinking. Jesus' brothers had been reared with Him, and to them He was simply an "older brother." When the time came to go up to Jerusalem to the feast of tabernacles, they chided Him for not making Himself manifest. "For even his brethren did not believe on him" (7:5). Intimacy may have dulled their insight and hindered true spiritual understanding of their brother's true mission.

It is possible for one to be reared under the sound of Jesus' teaching and in a home where religion is taken for granted and reach the point where he never gives serious thought to his faith. Nominally he does lip service to the teaching and to the Christ; but actually he never becomes a true believer to the degree demanded by Jesus and revealed in the Gospel of John. Intimacy may hinder belief.

Fear and Moral Cowardice

There is a venom about fear that too often paralyzes men. Some fear what others may think or what may be the consequences of their faith; others fear an attitude taken toward them; still others fear their weakness and proneness to failure. Some fear the cost of discipleship, for the price is not always low; it may be very high.

When Jesus came up to the feast of tabernacles, the people sought Him, "Yet no man spake openly of him for fear of the Jews" (7:13). Fear made them timid in seeking Jesus or in asking about Him.

The parents of the man born blind would not concede that Jesus had healed their son but said, "how he now seeth, we know not; or who opened his eyes, we know not: ask him; he is of age; he shall speak for himself. These things said his parents, because they feared the Jews: for the Jews had agreed already, that if any man should confess him to be Christ, he should be put out of the synagogue" (9:21-22). Fear made them think that they could not afford to believe. How many today are held back by the same power! Fear is a tyrant that chains man, holding him back, restraining him from being true to his own conscience and convictions.

With many, moral cowardice stands in the way of belief. Lack of the moral courage to express a conviction, to face the crowd of scoffers, or to stem the tide of those militantly opposed to supernatural interposition into the world has been a gigantic stumbling block. Pilate stands as a classic example of this type of hearer.

After Pilate had heard from the Jews their accusation of Jesus and had heard from Jesus Himself the type of kingdom He represented and the nature of His kingship, the governor knew the accusers had no case. His verdict to the Jews was, "I find no crime in him" (18:38). He then offered to release to them whomsoever they wished, offering a choice between Jesus and Barabbas, a robber. In making this offer Pilate thought they would relieve him of the responsibility of making the decision by choosing the release of Jesus. The governor was disappointed; they cried for Barabbas to be released instead of Jesus. Pilate tried another trick; he scourged Jesus and presented Him to them in a crown of platted thorns and the mock apparel of a king, saying again, "I find no crime in him" (19:1-4). Again his verdict was refused and rejected by the Jews. A third time Pilate thought to avoid the responsibility of putting an innocent man to death by telling them to take Him themselves and put Him to death, "for I find no crime in him" (19:6). But the Jews were not to be outwitted by this man whom they knew to be a moral coward. Their persistence carried the day, and Pilate's final verdict was to deliver Him unto them to be crucified (19:16).

Here is the picture of a moral coward, a man who knew what the evidence supported but who lacked the moral courage to accept the consequence of the evidence. This same weakness has hindered many from accepting the conclusion of the evidence and confessing that Jesus is the Christ, the Son of God. It takes courage to stand with one whose sole *forte* is truth and reliance upon spiritual power and who is opposed by the prejudice of religious tradition and by the intelligencia.

Misplaced Love

1. Lack of the love of God in their hearts

Probably a lack of the love of God is the real basis for the following three conditions; for in connection with the subject of praise and glory, Jesus stated this as the condition for unbelief of the Jews in Jerusalem. Having stated His claims that grew out of His relation to the Father and of the testimony of the Father to support those claims (ch. 5), Jesus said of Himself, "I receive not glory from men" (5:41). He proceeded from there to state the basic cause for their rejection of the testimony: "But I know you, that ye have not the love of God in yourselves" (5:42). He next charged them, "How can ye believe, who receive glory one of another, and the glory that cometh from the only God ye seek not?" (5:44). When this love of God does not exist in one's heart, he is not concerned with the praise of God that comes from doing His will. Instead of the love of God, there is love for the praise of men and love of the world.

2. Love of darkness

Jesus said, "He that believeth not hath been judged already, because he hath not believed on the name of the only begotten Son of God." But what is the basis of this judgment against unbelief and of the unbelief itself? "And this is the judgment, that the light is come into the world, and men loved the darkness rather than the light; for their works were evil. For everyone that doeth evil hateth the light, and cometh not to the light, lest his works should be reproved" (3:19-20). Unless one will allow the love of God to prepare the ground of His heart that he may overcome the love for evil, there is no hope for that one. The evidence falls only on a deaf ear and a wayside hearer so long as the individual loves the darkness and its works. The tragic history of Judas, when he bargained with the Jews to betray his Master for a few shekels of silver, has been repeated in the hearts of many since that day.

3. Love of the glory of men

Another love that holds some in unbelief is the love for human glory. Human glory and the honor one man may bestow upon another has a tremendous power over weak and fallible man. As Jesus preached and made an appeal from the words of Isaiah, some were so impressed that it is said, "Even of the rulers many believed on him; but because of the Pharisees they did not confess it, lest they should be put out of the synagogue: for they loved the glory that is of men more than the glory that is of God" (12:42-43). Had it been popular to accept and confess the Christ, had the Pharisees given the nod of approval to such, these would have gladly confessed. But it was unpopular to believe on Him, so they could not afford to let it be known that actually they did believe the evidence. These men were moral cowards; they looked for the praise of men—praise or glory of the wrong kind, from the wrong source. How many today stand in the shoes of these rulers? How many are afraid because they would become unpopular if it were known that they believe?

4. Love of self and material things

In this we have another misplaced love; self and things are placed above truth. Although Judas had been with Jesus from the time He selected those whom He called apostles, he seems not to have been impressed with the life of Jesus, with His teaching, or with His signs. John disdains to mention the sum received by Judas for betraying Jesus into the hands of His enemies but prefers to emphasize the fact that Jesus had known from the beginning who it was that should betray Him (6:64, 71; 12:4; 13:11), that the betrayal was inspired by Satan (13:2), and that the betrayer was one whom Jesus had chosen and who had eaten bread with Him (13:18). John preferred to give emphasis to the demeanor of Jesus in the presence of such a dastardly act. He discussed without rancor the betrayal (13:21-30), and presents Jesus as one who made no effort to hide Himself from Judas but who went to the customary place of prayer (18:1-3). He prefers to present the reaction of Jesus in the calm dignity He manifested in the presence of Judas and the soldiers as they came for Him (18:4-11). John sought to give emphasis to the testimony of Jesus' conduct as evidence to His deity rather than to the price Judas received. However, John does show that Judas was unimpressed by the evidence and hardened by his love for money to the point that he was willing to betray Jesus for whatever he might get out of the bargain. The love of money may so harden one that the evidence makes no impression.

The Hardened and Prejudiced Heart

When the eyes are willfully closed to evidence, the heart becomes hardened against the truth. The very evidence intended to open the eyes may leave one blind, and the truth that should soften and mellow the heart may in turn harden it. Because the teaching of Jesus and the signs He did among them made no impression for good upon the Jerusalem Jews, they refused to be honest in their evaluation of either; they could not believe. In this the words of Isaiah were fulfilled, "He hath blinded their eyes, and he hardened their heart; Lest they should see with their eyes, and perceive with their heart, and should turn" (12:37-40). A lack of disposition to hear and to see had led to a hardening of the heart which made it impossible morally—not arbitrarily—for them to believe even when stronger impulses were brought to bear upon them. The words of the psalmist are fitting: "Today, oh that ye would hear his voice! Harden not your heart, as at Meribah, As in the days of Massah in the wilderness; When your fathers tempted me, Proved me, and saw my work" (Ps. 95:7-9).

These unbelieving Jews were hardened by prejudice; others were hardened by brutality. The soldiers who were accustomed to such scenes as that of the crucifixion of Jesus had become hardened to such events. They were unimpressed by Jesus' words or behavior.

They parted His garments among themselves and then cast lots for the robe. John does not mention, as did Mark, the centurion's words, "Truly this man was the Son of God" (Mark 15:39). The centurion was impressed by the way Jesus had died, though apparently he had not heard Jesus teach. Hardened men are seldom impressed with the evidence and rarely pause to give it consideration. However, here was one who was an exception.

The saying, "None is so blind as is he who will not see," is fully exemplified in the Pharisees. They were so completely blinded by their prejudices for traditions that they could not see the power exerted by Jesus in the miracles He worked in their presence. When Jesus healed the man who had been a cripple for thirty-eight years, the Pharisees could see only that Jesus had violated their tradition of the sabbath. The facts that a fellow man was made whole and restored to usefulness in society, that a mighty act had been wrought that could have been effected only by divine power, and that some strange force of oppression had been overcome were utterly hidden from their view. They were completely blinded by their prejudice for a tradition. They demonstrated a total lack of spiritual and intellectual honesty.

The same was true when sight was restored to the man born blind, who from birth had lived in a state of darkness (ch. 9). One who possessed a divine power had anointed his eyes with clay and had told him to go to the pool of Siloam and wash. A simple faith led him to obey, and he came seeing. Why should not such an act of love, mercy, power, and authority have led all who beheld to rejoice and give glory to God? The answer: the act was on the sabbath and violated the traditions of the Pharisees. Immediately an inquisition began in an effort to bring to judgment the one who had performed the deed. Blinded by prejudice for traditions, a prejudice that knew no bounds, the Pharisees cast out of their communion the one on whom the miracle had been wrought. A mighty act had led to the conversion of only one man, while at the same time it led to the hardening of hundreds of others.

As Jesus beheld the contrast between the man made to see, who returned to kneel at the feet of Jesus and worship, and the Pharisees, so blind in their prejudices, He was made to say, "For judgment came I into this world, that they that see not may see; and that they that see may become blind" (v. 39). The man formerly blind could now see, both physically and spiritually; the

Pharisees, who could see physically, were now spiritually blind. When they heard the statement of Jesus, they asked, "Are we also blind?" To this question Jesus replied, "If ye were blind, ye would have no sin: but now ye say, We see: your sin remaineth" (vv. 40-41). Is it not true that today many who say, "We see," are blinded by their prejudice for traditions to the point that they cannot see the truth as it is in Jesus, and so remain in their sin?

A basic necessity for proper consideration of evidence is the honest heart. The heart must be disposed to give a fair and impartial hearing of evidence in any matter. As one reads the Gospel of John, he can feel that the rulers, blinded by prejudice and love for human glory, were dishonest with the evidence that Jesus presented. The Jews brought the woman who had been taken in adultery to Jesus, not because they were interested in either the law of Moses or a proper sense of justice, but that they might try Him, "that they might have whereof to accuse him" (8:6). Their dishonesty was further displayed in their admission, "for this man doeth many signs" (11:47); but in spite of the acknowledgement of the signs, they were determined to put Him to death.

One wonders if there are not those today who reject the evidence because of lack of honesty in weighing the evidence. It is not for any to judge the motive of another, but it does behoove the one examining the evidence to ask himself the question, "Am I being fair with the evidence as that evidence stands out before me?" The man who deifies his own intellectual acumen will find it difficult to be fair with any evidence that points to the supernatural.

Intellectual Pride

This has been mentioned above as companion to dishonesty. The intellectual pride of the Pharisees expressed itself when they said to the officers sent to arrest Jesus, "Hath any of the rulers believed on him, or of the Pharisees?" (7:48). Here is expressed the pride of an ecclesiastical hierarchy. Until the rulers have believed on Him, do others have ground on which to believe? The hierarchy, controlled by an intellectual pride that would enslave the minds of the common people, deem it right to dictate that which others are to believe and not to believe. This disposition will hinder belief by men who are dominated by it, and fear will hinder belief by those under the control of the hierarchy. "Nevertheless even of the rulers many believed on him; but because of the Pharisees they did not confess it, lest they should be put out of the synagogue: for they loved the glory that is of men more than the glory that is of God" (12:42-43). Intellectual pride goes hand in hand with dishonesty; and at the same time, subjection to and fear of an intellectual hierarchy go hand in hand. All these are hindrances to a fair evaluation of evidence and are contributing features to unbelief.

Indifference

Finally there is that intangible thing called indifference which stands in the way of belief. John deals with those who, in the light of the evidence presented, were impressed. Some became believers, ready and willing to die with the Lord. Others became bitter enemies, ready to persecute to the death those who should believe. God had come into the world in the person of His Son to divide the world into these two categories. Between these two groups there are always those who, with a shrug of the shoulders, say, "So what!" and go their way. Doubtless in Jesus' day there were many of these who were interested in the signs as passive observers of that which for the moment entertained, but who lacked the depth of concern or interest to make a decision either for or against Jesus. This class merits no mention. They would not enter into the picture as either hot or cold, so they would be spewed out as unworthy of mention either way. Indifference indicates a lack of honesty which hinders the desire and search for truth.

Conclusion

Truly, a marvelous and unique character has been among the sons of men! He is one who cannot be ignored. Everyone who comes in contact with Jesus must take a position concerning His being.

He possessed and displayed a knowledge of God and of spiritual matters that combines and transcends all that had been known of deity through the past ages. He revealed this knowledge in teaching and in action. He made men see and grasp a new concept of the Almighty.

He so exposed the sophistry of religious bigots and hypocrites that they crucified Him. When they failed to answer His teaching, which laid bare the emptiness of their traditions, and were made to smart under the complete exposure of their dishonesty, they determined to put Him to death and turned Him over to the cowardly Roman governor for execution. The exposure was the crushing defeat of all religious error and the failure of tradition to stand the fiery test of truth.

The charge of this one, "which of you convicteth me of sin?" was not met then and has continued unmet until this day. Brilliant philosophers have attempted to meet the challenge, but each has had to face the shame of failure. He neither transgressed the teaching of the law nor violated the principles of His own doctrine. He stands and has stood before the world as man's one sinless fellow being.

The temple guard testified, "Never man so spake"; and Jesus so impressed Pilate, the Roman governor, that he was forced to confess, "I find no crime in him." To this testimony can be added that of the Roman centurion, "Truly, this was the Son of God." This was the impression He made on unbelievers.

This unique man promised that He would send the Holy Spirit from God who would guide the apostles into all the truth. Moved by this Spirit, they were able to reveal the mystery of previous ages—God's plan for human redemption. Since the apostles completed their work, not one iota of spiritual and moral truth has been added to their revelation of God's will as summed up in Jesus. All the modern so-called inspiration and new revelation has added nothing to the body of truth which we possess. If what is claimed to be a new revelation is true, it can be found already revealed in the Bible, therefore it is not new. If such new teachings are not true, the teachings of Christ and the apostles contradict the new. If it is true, it is not new; if it is new, it is not true. In Jesus Christ the revelation of the spiritual and moral truth reached its final apex and complete fulness.

The life and message of this one has changed the world. Through Him and His message woman has been lifted to her proper place of dignity and the home made a heaven on earth. When He and His teaching are rejected in the home, a hell on earth follows. Society in general is given an ideal toward which to strive, and through this Jesus, flavor is given to life. Through Him business has been given a standard of integrity and honor that lifts it above suspicion and corruption when that teaching is followed. When His teaching is rejected, an economy ultimately collapses under the weight of its own wickedness and evil doing.

Above these, this one has given to groveling humanity a dignity that lifts it to heights heretofore unknown. His message brings peace to the troubled soul and fills it with a true and permanent joy. It points the sin-weary pilgrim to the abundant life here, and beyond this to a life that is eternal with God. Jesus Christ answers the longing of the hungry soul as He fills that soul with Himself, the bread of life, and assures the traveler that the life He offers looks to eternal life.

The evidence has been presented. The man and His teaching are before all. Every individual must weigh the evidence, examine his own life, and deduce a judgment. Either Jesus is what He claimed to be, or He is the world's unexplained enigma.

With the stakes so high and eternity so vast, can one afford to gamble with his soul? An honest and fair investigation is worth all that it demands, and this is what Jesus asks. In the time of Jesus and during the centuries since, many have searched and found assurance and peace, reaching the conclusion of the Roman centurion, "Truly, this was the Son of God." It is to be hoped that the reader of this book will reach the same conclusion, and in the firm confidence of faith will find the joy of salvation in Jesus, the Christ, the Son of the living God!

Bibliography

Commentaries

Alford, Henry. *The Greek Testament*. London: Rivingtons, Waterloo Place, 1859.

Barclay, Wm. *The Gospel of John* (2 vols). Philadelphia: The
Westminster Press, 1956.

Dods, Marcus. *The Gospel of St. John. Expositor's Greek Testament, Vol. I*, Grand Rapids: Wm. B. Eerdmans Pub. Co.,
undated.

Eerdman, Chas. R. *The Gospel of John*. Philadelphia: The Westminster Press, 1949.

Hendriksen, Wm. *New Testament Commentary: Exposition of the
Gospel According to John* (2 vols). Grand Rapids: Baker Book
House, 1953.

Johnson, B. W. *John—N. T. Commentary*. St. Louis: Christian
Publishing Co., 1886.

Keil, Carl and Delitzsch, Franz. *Biblical Commentary on the Old
Testament* (25 vols). Reprint. Grand Rapids: Wm. B. Eerdmans,
1949.

Lenski, R. C. H. *The Interpretation of St. John's Gospel*. Colum-
bus: The Wartburg Press, 1942.

Lightfoot, J. B. *St. Paul's Epistle to the Colossians and to Philemon.* Eighth edition. New York: MacMillan & Company, 1886.

Reynolds, H. R. *Pulpit Commentary* (51 vols), *The Gospel of St. John* (2 vols). New York: Funk and Wagnalls Co., undated.

Westcott, B. F. *The Gospel According to St. John.* Grand Rapids: Wm. B. Eerdmans Publishing Company, 1950.

Encyclopedias and Lexicons

Arndt, Wm. F. and Gingrich, F. Wilbur. *A Greek-English Lexicon of the New Testament.* Chicago: University of Chicago Press, 1952 ed.

Thayer, Wm. Henry. *Grimms Greek-English Lexicon.* New York: American Book Co., 1886 Harper Bros.

Vincent, Marvin R. *Word Studies in the New Testament.* Grand Rapids: Wm. B. Eerdmans Pub. Co., 1946.

Vine, W. E. *An Expository Dictionary of New Testament Words* (4 vols). London: Oliphants Limited, 1940.

General

Harrison, Everett F. *Baker's Dictionary of Theology.* Grand Rapids: Baker Book House, 1960.

McGarvey, J. W. *Evidences of Christianity.* Cincinnati: Guide Printing and Publishing Co., 1886.

Orr, Jas. (ed.). *International Standard Bible Encyclopedia* (5 vols). Grand Rapids: Wm. B. Eerdmans Pub. Co., 1949.

Robertson, A. T. *The Divinity of Christ in the Gospel of John.* New York: Fleming H. Revell Co., 1916.

Tenney, Merrill C. *John: The Gospel of Belief.* Grand Rapids: Wm. B. Eerdmans Pub. Co., 1948.

Tidwell, Josiah Blake. *John and His Five Books.* Grand Rapids: Wm. B. Eerdmans Pub. Co., 1937.

Trench, R. C. *Notes on the Miracles of Our Lord.* Grand Rapids: Baker Book House, 1954.

Vos, Geerhardus. *The Self-Disclosure of Jesus.* Grand Rapids: Wm. B. Eerdmans, 1954.